Praise for *Dead End*

"Bob has done an incredible job of in-depth investigating the I 70 murders. This book takes the readers back to the crime scenes and presents many previously unknown details about the investigators and agencies involved. More importantly, this book serves as a way of preserving case information while ensuring families of the victims, that every person associated with these cases cares deeply, has and will continue to remember these young victims."

—**Michael Crooke**, Indianapolis Police Department

"For those of us in police service who have lived and worked on this case for more than 30 years, we will never stop pursuing this case. From the beginning, we have sought the public's help in finding this serial killer through the release of appropriate information about the case. Bob's book will help us continue our pursuit."

—**Pat McCarrick**, St. Charles Police Department

"Trish was more than a wife. She was my best friend, the love of my life. Over the years I have kept up on her case. I owe this to her to participate in any way I can. I have the deepest appreciation for Bob's book that may draw the public's attention, hopefully reaching someone that might help bring this murderer to justice."

—**Mark Magers**, husband of Patricia Magers

"Thanks for shedding light on this case, Bob. You have been a breath of fresh air and I know if this case gets solved it will be in part because of you and your dogged determination to help us seek the truth."

—**Brad Rumsey**, Terre Haute Police Department

DEAD END

Inside The Hunt For The I-70 Serial Killer

Bob Cyphers

Genius
Book Publishing

Milwaukee Wisconsin USA

Published by:
Genius Book Publishing
PO Box 250380
Milwaukee Wisconsin 53225
GeniusBookPublishing.com

ISBN: 978-1-958727-21-8

231229 HQ

Have you seen this man?

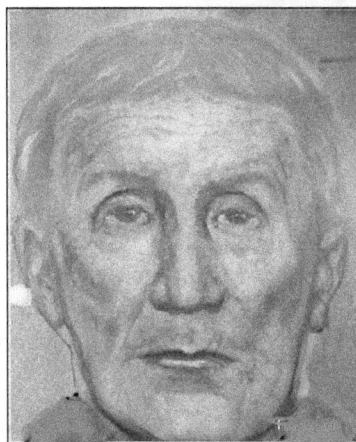

To the determined police detectives in Indianapolis, Wichita, Terre Haute, St. Charles, and Raytown. You have never stopped. My respect for you is enormous.

Acknowledgments

To my wife Alison, who kept insisting that I keep writing to help find the killer; to Terry Coley and Linda Green for making sure my participles are not dangling; and to my children Christian, Austin and Dylan who kept cheering dad on to get this book to the public.

Foreword

by Captain Raymond Floyd,
St. Charles, Missouri Police Department

In 1992 I remember hearing about a murder, which occurred in St. Charles at Boot Village. It seemed very quickly investigators were able to link this murder with those in Indianapolis, Wichita, Terre Haute, and Raytown. The media dubbed the suspect as the I-70 serial killer. As time passed, the case seemed to vanish from the media, almost as quickly as it started. Once in a while, I would catch a story of new information being shared by the investigators, but no arrests were ever made.

I immediately started reading every report and file the Police Department had on the case. I was very impressed by the St. Charles Police and the previous investigators, who worked this case. This case never went cold in St.

Charles and investigators had followed up on numerous leads since the original murder. With that said, it looked like it had been approximately 15 years since all agencies involved had taken a good hard look at the case. With the advancement of DNA, I thought this would be an ideal time to crack the case wide open.

I contacted Indianapolis, Wichita, Terre Haute, and Raytown about meeting. I got buy-in from all involved agencies. In addition, we contacted our federal partners, as well as DNA experts. We also wanted to get media involvement and our choice was Bob Cyphers with KMOV-TV. The cases were discussed in detail, the evidence was reviewed, and an investigative strategy was formulated. In addition, Mr. Cyphers did an excellent job of profiling the case in local media. He actually completed a series consisting of seven episodes and titled, "Chasing the I-70 Serial Killer." This exposure eventually led to national exposure of the case by People Magazine Investigates on the Discovery Channel.

We have and continue to test numerous items associated with the murders perpetrated by the I-70 killer. Although I cannot comment about the evidence, we remain optimistic about solving the crime. Equally important is continuing to share the information and keeping the story alive in the public. I do believe there is a great possibility of a witness coming forward after hearing the story of the I-70 killer. This book will help ensure the story stays alive and maybe it will trigger a memory of someone reading it about a potential suspect. I would encourage anyone who may have information to contact our hotline at 1-800-800-3510.

xii

Introduction

I thought about the Nancy Kitzmiller case many times over the years. As a much younger reporter, I was there that horrible summer day some 30 years ago when Nancy's body was discovered inside the Boot Village store in St. Charles, a suburb west of St. Louis. I continued to follow the police investigation closely over the years as it turned into a serial killer case, and then into a cold case. And then an ice cold case.

Time went by, and Nancy's murder was now just a memory. And then one day the phone rang. St. Charles police detectives were launching a task force, bringing together investigators from Indianapolis, Wichita, Terre Haute, and Kansas City, the other locations where the serial killer struck small stores in strip malls along Interstate 70 in 1992. Thirty years after the killer's spree, with advancements in technology and DNA, they would gather to try to track down the killer one last time. It would be a full court press.

"We are going to give this one more shot," said Captain Raymond Floyd of the St. Charles Police Department. "Are you interested in telling our story?"

"You bet I am," I answered.

"Good," Floyd said. "We start in two weeks."

"Is it really possible?" I asked Floyd. "I mean, 30 years is an awfully long time. And I know there really has never been a solid lead in Nancy's case, or in any of the other cases."

Floyd heard the doubt in my voice. A veteran police officer always chooses his words carefully. "Yes, I do think it is possible," Floyd said. "You will see us go after this guy with everything we have. Everything. FBI, DNA, profilers, everything. You are with us?"

"I am with you," I said.

"Good," he said. "Pack a suitcase. You will follow the footsteps of the killer."

With that, we were off and running. Everyone would meet in St. Louis to share notes, then head back to their respective communities. In the days to follow, I would join them. Their stories, as horrific as they are, and their dogged pursuit of a madman decades later, follow in the pages ahead.

CHAPTER 1
"And then I started wondering, was Robin really the first? Could there have been others before her?"

The phone rings every April 8 in Susan Fuldauer's Indianapolis home. She will pause what she is doing, look at the incoming number, glance quickly at the calendar, and smile. Mike Crooke never, ever forgets.

"I just pick up the phone every April 8 and I call her," Crooke says. "And I say to her 'Hey Susan, I am not calling you because I have some good news to report about.' It is more like 'Hey Susan, I have not forgotten about you, your family or your sister Robin, and I never will. I am still out here plugging away. I am still out here trying to do my best.' I always call her on the anniversary of that day and just remind her that she and her family are still in my thoughts, and they always will be."

Crooke, the longtime sergeant of the Indianapolis Police Department, has remembered since April 8, 1992, the day the Robin Fuldauer nightmare began. He is long since retired, but he has never, ever forgotten.

ℰℐ

November 2021. Our crew left St. Louis in the early morning and headed east, photographer Chuck Delaney driving, producer JJ Bailey riding shotgun, and me in the backseat taking notes of the scenery along Interstate 70. As we drive along the highway I picture in my mind what the killer saw 30 years ago. Pick an exit to get off, quickly find a small store in a strip mall, make sure a woman is working alone, get in and get out without being seen, and leave a body behind. Surely it is not that easy. It simply can't be.

Our first stop, like the killer's, was Indianapolis. Interstate 70 east through Indy to the 465 loop, then a quick jaunt north. The killer wasn't patient, he took the first possible exit, Pendleton Pike. He could have headed east or west. He could have picked any woman, anywhere, to kill. He chose to turn left at the light and go west. And then he immediately had options to kill on both his right and left. He picked the Payless shoe store.

The Indianapolis police detectives still working the Robin Fuldauer case were waiting for us when we arrived. Like other major cities, Indianapolis had seen a huge spike in homicide cases recently. Their staff was spread thin trying to solve not only murders that seemed to be happening daily, but cold cases that had piled up over the years. Clearance rates, or rates of solving homicides, ranged around 50 percent. That meant hundreds of unsolved cases piled up each year. After 30 years, an unsolved homicide is often a file, in a box, in a closet, never to be opened again.

"We have thousands of unsolved cases over the years," said Captain Roger Spurgeon of the Indianapolis Police Department. "And more are coming every week. It is overwhelming. You do the best you can do, and then another case lands on your desk."

Spurgeon and I looked around the busy Pendleton Pike area and I knew we were reading each other's minds: The killer could have stopped anywhere.

"Why here, do you think?" I voiced to the detectives. "He could have stopped anywhere. Why do you think he stopped here?"

The men looked at each other and shook their heads. A question that has never been answered here, or at any of the other crime scenes.

"This would be one of the last places you would think he would strike," said Columbus Ricks, one of the Indianapolis detectives. "Look at how busy this area is."

But Spurgeon guessed there was a method in the killer's madness. "I think there would have been a variety of stores for him to choose from in the area," Spurgeon said. "It was just a matter of whatever our suspect was looking for at the time. You have all of this busy traffic around this area, all of this movement, all of these people coming and going so quickly. Unless somebody really stood out to someone as behaving oddly or looking oddly, you could really go about your business with relative anonymity and nobody would ever really pay you any attention."

I pointed to the busy Speedway gas station that was literally steps from the Payless shoe store. Customers were filling their tanks, and numerous people were coming and going inside the store by the minute.

"Was the gas station there in 1992?" I asked Spurgeon. He nodded yes.

"That does not make any sense," I said. "You would have to be a fool to kill somebody with this many potential witnesses around."

Ricks and fellow detective David Ellison both laughed.

Spurgeon nodded again. "Welcome to the world of the I-70 serial killer where nothing makes any sense."

I walked up to the front door of the gas station, and then took a few steps to the Payless store. It took me less than 20 seconds. Ellison and Ricks stood alongside Spurgeon and watched me make the walk.

"Twenty seconds," I hollered at them. "No way somebody is killing somebody with all of these people just 20 seconds away."

I looked at Spurgeon again. He nodded and I shook my head. "No way," I muttered to myself.

I kept walking between the gas station and shoe store, and then returned to the detectives.

"Let me make sure I have this right," I said. "He somehow chooses this busy location in the middle of the day. Then he kills Robin with all these people around. And then what, he just disappears?"

"Pretty much," said Ellison. "Pretty much."

Robin Fuldauer was not sure where life was taking her yet, but she was moving very quickly. She was the salutatorian of her Lawrence Central High School class, located just down the street from the Payless shoe store. She graduated a few years later from Indiana University. And now she had already risen to become a manager for Payless.

Sometime around 1pm on that April day, a serial killer was about to embark on a month-long journey, one that would take him to five cities, leaving six body bags behind. He was patrolling Pendleton Pike Road, looking for his first victim.

Receipts from the store show the last purchase was made at 1:12pm. Police believe the killer was likely in the store at the time, saw the only other customer leave, and then made his move. He forced Fuldauer into a storage room in the back of the store, made her kneel, then shot her twice in the back of the head, execution style, with a .22 caliber handgun. There was no sign of any struggle inside the store. The killer then rummaged through the cash register, taking less than $100. Police believe he left through a back door by 1:30pm, leaving Fuldauer lying dead behind a closed door. For the next hour, Payless customers would have their run of the store, with nobody in sight.

"I don't believe there was an opportunity for anybody to go inside the store and observe that there was a body there," Spurgeon said.

The Payless store had little in the way of store security. Just a bell that would ring when a new customer arrived.

Police records showed a woman named Lucretia Gullett was working at the Speedway gas station the day Fuldauer was killed. It was Gullett who discovered Robin's body and called police.

Before arriving in Indianapolis, I began the task of searching for Lucretia Gullet.

"Is this Lucretia Gullet?" I asked the woman on the other end of the phone.

"It is," she said.

"Ma'am," I said, "I am a reporter working on a serial killer from 1992. And I believe you found the body of his first victim. A woman named Robin Fuldauer in the Payless shoe store."

Gullett paused on the other end. "I did not really find her body. But yes, I was there, and I called the police. But what did you say about a serial killer?"

I told Gullett her Payless killer went on to kill numerous other women across the country.

"What?!" she screamed into the phone.

And I realized she was unaware. "Do you still live around Indy?" I asked her.

"I do," she said.

"I am coming to town," I told her. "Would you meet with me?"

"I will," she said. "And did you say serial killer?" Apparently, she was still coming to grips with this.

I stood by the Speedway gas station with my crew and the police detectives, and watched as a woman parked her car and walked toward us.

"I am looking for Bob," she said.

"Hi Lucretia," I said, and we shook hands.

We began walking around the area. "This brings back a lot of memories," she said.

"Have you been back here since…?" I asked.

"No," she said as she looked around. "Thirty years is a long time. I just avoided coming around here."

I asked Gullett to take me back to that day, as best she could.

"My shift at the Speedway gas station was ending at 3pm. I was almost getting off work to go home when I received a phone call from a man who said he was the district manager of the Payless store. It was probably around 2pm," Gullett remembered. "He told me that he had been calling the shoe store for quite a while, but that no one was answering the phone there. He was really concerned, so I told him I would go next door to Payless and see what was going on over there."

Gullett and I made the 20 second walk from one store to the other. "What happened when you walked in?" I asked.

Gullett paused at the door. "This is hard," she said. "I walked up to the front door, opened it up and looked around. I did not see anybody. No manager, no customers. I looked over to the left and noticed that the cash register was open and then I went through the aisles, but nobody was around. I really was not sure what was going on, but I knew it was not right. Then I heard someone talking in the back of the store, so I went back there and I saw a woman who had a child with her. They were looking at some shoes. I asked her to please leave, and told her something was wrong. I did not know what was happening, but I knew something was wrong. So I just immediately stopped looking around and called the police. I was probably only in the store for about 10 minutes. And then I just waited for the police to arrive."

Police records show they arrived at the scene around 3pm. When they did, Gullett said she then stood watch over the front door while detectives made their way inside. She watched them search the store before heading towards the back. And then she saw them open a closed door and look inside.

"One officer looked down to the right," Gullett said, "and I could tell he was shocked at what he saw."

Incredibly, some 30 years after Robin Fuldauer was murdered, Gullett says she was not aware the homicide scene she walked into three decades ago became linked to a serial killer, or that it was not solved all these years earlier. "I just became aware of that when you called me," she said.

"You did not follow the case over the years as it exploded?" I asked.

"No," she said. "I was shocked when you told me it was a serial killer. I was like, whoa! That is when I put two and two together, and like, wow!"

Brought back to the scene, and meeting new detectives for the first time. Gullett is now spending time detailing the case to police again.

"They wanted to know if there was anything else I ever came up with or thought about." And then she winked and smiled. "Maybe. Maybe. It might just be a coincidence. But yes, I hope I can help."

☙

Roger Spurgeon was an Indianapolis police officer at the time of Robin Fuldauer's murder, not yet working in homicide. Now, he has been with the police department more than 25 years, most of them in the homicide unit. He would inherit the Fuldauer case, and says that in spite of the busy area, and in spite of the busy time of the day, early leads in the case quickly fizzled. "At first, because there was a small amount of cash taken, detectives thought it was likely a robbery that somehow turned into a homicide. They had a variety of potential suspects they were looking at in the very beginning. But If you describe a suspect as somebody you really have a keen interest in because of some sort of an evidentiary link or eyewitnesses, no, there was nothing there which stood out to the investigators at that time."

Detectives immediately began canvassing the area on Pendleton Pike. The first witness they found was the store manager at MAB paint, across the street from the Payless, He told police he saw a strange looking man carrying a long bag. The witness said he watched the man repeatedly circling the Payless store, and then watched as the man sat down at a curb nearby for nearly 30 minutes. And then around 2pm, he suddenly disappeared from sight. The witness told police the man appeared to either be on drugs or had a mental problem.

Police would only locate less than a half dozen potential witnesses. One of them said they saw a man who matched what the earlier witness said calmly trying to hitch a ride along the highway. Police found a couple of other witnesses in the area who thought they saw something, but none of those leads panned out.

Detective Columbus Ricks is part of the Indianapolis Unsolved Homicide Unit. Like Spurgeon, he was also an Indianapolis police officer at the time of the Fuldauer murder. "The homicide investigators tracked down almost everybody that was said to have seen something in the area or had been seen by someone. They all had enough of an alibi to eliminate them. The descriptions of the suspect were all black males…" Ricks said, shaking his head. "And within days, after Wichita, the detectives knew the killer was a white male."

I looked at Ricks and laughed. "How stupid," I said.

"Not as easy as it seems on TV," Ricks laughed again.

And then came the question: How did the killer get away? How did he simply walk out of the store in the middle of the day, with people all around, and disappear into thin air?

"I think he could have easily parked a vehicle on one of these residential side streets and casually walked to it," Spurgeon said. "And nobody would have paid any attention to him unless he was acting strangely. Obviously, he had to have some sort of wheels to get from point A to point B. But we still do not have a good handle on that. Detectives had a lot of different theories at the time."

Our crew walked around the area near the store. Busy streets in front, a side street on the side, and an older residential section behind it. Spurgeon appeared to be on target. The most likely answer was the killer parked a car on one of the residential streets, walked calmly to the Payless store, murdered Robin Fuldauer, and then walked back to his car.

Time moves forward. Today, a Batteries Plus store sits where the Payless Shoe store stood in 1992. But what has not changed is that police departments in five cities are still digging, talking to each other, and hoping for a DNA match.

"Science was not as developed then as it is now," said Ricks. "We are going to see if DNA and new technology can assist us in solving this case." Ricks added that another new witness may have recently emerged. Until then, we wait. The police. The families. Everyone. And they all understand that they are waiting for an answer that may never come.

Robin's sister Susan will never forget that day. You can still hear the sadness in her voice. "My husband found out about Robin first. He came home and told me. It was just so incredibly hard to process. It was something completely out of the realm of expectations. I immediately went to pick up my daughter and then we went to the Payless store. There was so much activity at the scene it was hard to believe. It is just a nightmare that you live through and cannot possibly process. It is just very hard to describe."

And then just a few days later, the bombshell of Wichita came, where 700 miles away and just three days after Robin Fuldauer was murdered, Patricia Magers and Patricia Smith were killed in the same fashion. And almost immediately, police were hit with a stunning reality: The same gun used in Indianapolis was used in Wichita. It seemed impossible with the time frame. But, suddenly, Indianapolis and Wichita had a serial killer on their hands.

"Then it all became just surreal," Susan said. "Wichita was connected to my Robin? And again, look at the pattern. So cold blooded. Another busy, noisy store. And then the others soon came rolling in. And then I started wondering, was Robin really the first? Could there have been others before her? This was now totally beyond belief. And then our family began grieving not just for

Robin, but for all of these other families going through the same exact nightmare that we were going through."

There is another heartbreaking twist of fate to Robin's story. She was not supposed to work that day, but another employee called in sick. The Payless store was short-staffed, so Robin came in to cover the shift, as she had so many times before.

After all these years, one thought keeps sticking in Susan's mind. "I know you cannot turn the clock back. But I usually went by Robin's store on most days after I got off of work, just to make sure she was okay. For some reason, I did not go by that day. And I always ask myself, 'Could I have possibly done something? Could I have possibly stopped something?'"

Susan Fuldauer is realistic about the chances of finding the killer after all these years. But she says she will always remain hopeful. "We have always maintained hope that Robin's murder will someday be solved. Maybe the killer is in jail somewhere. Maybe he is no longer alive. But, like the detectives tell us, we have new technology now. We have new DNA techniques. We have hope. It does not bring Robin or the other victims back. But to know that he might be stopped, and he can never do anything like this again, that would be a major victory for our family."

Mike Crooke, who has seen everything in his 52 years in law enforcement, insists the case can someday be solved. "I am still hopeful we will resolve this. We did not have the advances in science 30 years ago that we have now."

Robin Fuldauer was 26 years old. She was the first known victim of the I-70 serial killer. And while it all began in Indy, sadly, it did not end there. And on April 8, pick a year, any year, Mike Crooke will pick up the phone and call Susan Fuldauer. She will smile. They will talk. And they will cry. "It is so kind and considerate of Mike to reach out to my family," Susan said. "He reminds us that Robin will never ever be forgotten. I appreciate that so very much. We do not talk about the what ifs, because this was such a heinous crime. It is just very comforting to know that Mike remembers us each year. That amount of kindness is really wonderful and will never be forgotten."

CHAPTER 2
"How he picked this one is anybody's guess…"

Norman Smith woke up at 6am that Saturday morning in Wichita. He had a "Walk for Mankind" to participate in. He kissed his wife Patricia goodbye, knowing he would not see her until she got off work that evening at 6pm.

By 6:15pm, Patricia had not arrived home so Norman began cooking dinner. 6:30pm came, and still no Patricia. "That was odd," Smith said. "We only lived five minutes from her work. She was always home by then. I called the store. No answer. I waited 10 more minutes and called again. No answer."

Smith wasn't waiting any longer. "By 6:45pm, I was in the car and on my way. It just felt odd."

Odd quickly turned into something far worse. "There were people everywhere around the store. Police. Yellow crime tape. Just like in the movies."

Smith began desperately looking for answers. "I finally got to a police officer who would only tell me Patricia was at the hospital."

Smith paused for a long time, and I just waited.

"I was just in a state of shock. I was destroyed. I looked over at another man whose world appeared to be totally wrecked. And I immediately knew it must have been Patricia Magers' husband."

"That will be a very tough day for me," Mark Magers told me when I called him. "Very tough. But if you are coming all this way, I will be there. But it will not be easy."

Thirty years is a long time. But for Magers, it was yesterday. I told him I was coming to Wichita, working on the I-70 serial killer case, and asked if he could meet me at his wife's store. I arrived first, and watched as a man pulled into the parking lot and got out of his car.

Magers walked slowly, and I watched him look around the strip mall with a tight smile on his face. He would stop, pause, and stare. His wife's store, La Bride d'Elegance and Sir Knight Tuxedo and Formal Wear, sitting in a strip mall on East Kellogg Street, was long gone, but the strip mall still remained, anchored by a State Farm office, a family ministry, and a hair salon. I walked up to him and said hello. It took Magers a few minutes to gather his thoughts and speak.

"No hurry," I told him. "Look around. Take your time. And then try to take me back."

"The location here has certainly changed a lot over the 30 years," he said. "But the memories I have kept all these years have not changed a bit. I can still remember this place like it was that Saturday afternoon when I came over here."

As is often the case in homicides, Magers realized something was not right. "I was home cooking dinner. Patricia had not arrived home from work yet, and that was not like her. I called the store and there was no answer. So I paged her but she did not answer. That is when I got worried. I started calling around to her friends but nobody had seen or heard from her. I thought she might have had some sort of car trouble. So I got in my car and I came up here and then…" Magers voice trailed off for several moments before he continued, "And then I walked into a very, very chaotic scene. A living nightmare."

Magers then handed me an envelope with pictures of his wife, pictures that were now his most treasured memory. I knew this was difficult for him. We took our time and strolled outside the strip mall.

જી

It takes 10 hours and 15 minutes of highway driving along Interstate 70 through four states to make it from the Payless store in Indianapolis to the La Bride d'Elegance and Sir Knight Tuxedo and Formal Wear in Wichita. The odometer records 685 miles. There are numerous potential pit stops along the way, many with strip malls just off the interstate with females working alone. Effingham and Vandalia in Illinois. St. Louis and Columbia in Missouri. Ottawa and Emporia in Kansas. But none of those locations seemed to matter to a killer who was about to become a serial killer who seemed to be in a hurry to kill again.

Wichita Detective Tim Relph laughed when I told him I had driven from Indianapolis to Wichita to track the serial killer. "That is a long drive, brother."

"Same drive as the killer," I told him.

Where Roger Spurgeon has the formal buttoned up look of a police detective, Relph gives the impression of Peter Falk as Columbo stalking the case, a mastermind behind his glasses and khakis, information held close to his vest, waiting to pounce when a suspect least expects it.

I asked him what he thought when he first heard that the ballistics from Wichita matched those from Indianapolis.

He could only shake his head. "I just do not see somebody just wandering between here and Indy without a reason. You made that drive. I have made that drive. You have got to want to get here for something. Indy to Wichita is a long haul in two and a half days. I do not think he got in the car in Indy and decided 'I am going to go to Wichita and kill two people.' There are plenty of places between here and there he could have stopped that would have been much easier and simpler for him. And you know he had to stop along the way multiple times. We know he was not afraid of crowds. He did not have to come this far for this. You do not make that drive accidentally, especially branching off from Kansas City. Whatever happened in Indianapolis, this guy had to get on the road quickly to pull this off. He obviously traveled with a purpose. We just do not know what it was."

But whatever the killer's purpose was, it was about to quickly go off the rails. After killing Robin Fuldauer three days earlier in Indianapolis, the serial killer walked into a major problem in Wichita. Two of them. First, instead of one lone victim working at the La Bride d'Elegance and Sir Knight Tuxedo and Formal Wear store, the killer discovered there were two, Patricia Magers and Patricia Smith. Magers was the store owner, and Smith a part time employee. The store was due to close at 6pm, but a customer who was heading to a wedding called just before closing saying he needed a cummerbund for his tuxedo at the last minute. He was heading to the store, but did not know if he could make it there by 6pm. Was it possible, he asked, if they could please stay open a few extra minutes just in case he was late? Both women happily agreed to help him. That act of kindness would cost them their lives.

"It was right at closing time," said Relph. "For the killer, he probably has some knowledge when the store is supposed to be closing, so he can certainly time his attack.

First off, I do not think he ever expected two women to be in that store. And second, he had no way of knowing that a customer would soon be arriving moments after he did."

And when there was a knock on the door a few minutes after 6pm, Smith, working in the front of the store, went to open it, expecting to find the cummerbund customer. Instead, she stared into the eyes of her killer.

Mark Magers looked again to where his wife's store had been. He has replayed what the police have told him likely happened inside the store thousands of times over in his mind. "They think my wife was likely in the back doing business stuff. Patricia Smith was in the front, probably cleaning up. The killer would have then forcefully taken Smith into the back room where he would have been surprised to find my wife. We did not have much security in the store back then. We had a panic button installed in the front of the store, and we had run some practice drills with that, but the girls obviously did not have enough time to get to it."

Police say the killer made the women lay face down, then tied them up. He then shot Magers twice, Smith once, and prepared for a quick getaway out the front door. And then he faced his second problem: The cummerbund customer was now walking through the same door looking for assistance.

"He certainly did not expect a customer to come walking through the front door," Relph said. "He obviously thought the store was closed. It was after closing hours. The customer was a long way away from the killer, in the front of the store. The killer was still toward the back of the store. But the customer now stood between the killer and his ability to get out the front door. The killer certainly did not expect to be trapped in the store. He needed to go out the front door. There was no other way. He was trapped." Relph shook his head picturing that scene. "But with a gun in the killer's hand, so was the customer."

The cummerbund customer looked at the killer and saw the gun. The pair exchanged words. The killer told the man to go to the back room where he had the women tied up. The customer balked and began backing away toward the door. The killer then told him to get out and not say a word. The customer continued backing away slowly out the front door. He never turned his back to the killer. He left the store and fled.

Relph is surprised there were not three homicide victims at the store. "The situation certainly did not go as the killer had planned. Within the store he had the crime contained, but then once you have a witness come in, and then the witness is possibly going back out into the parking lot where other people are around, at some point you have to just cut it off and get the situation over with. The killer could not keep hanging around the store that much longer with those women in the back. If that witness would have cooperated with him and gone into the back room, he would have surely been a dead man.

There would have been no reason to let him live. But when the witness balked, the killer was clearly thinking fast on his feet, and decided not to shoot him. Because that witness, even wounded, if he makes it out of the front door alive, the whole thing blows up in public."

The witness, stunned and scared at what he just went through, ran from the store and waited about an hour before he called police. The 911 recording states the witness reported seeing only "an armed man approaching the store." That delay in time thwarted the investigators, who did not arrive until around 7:30pm, where they found the bodies of Magers and Smith in a pool of blood. Magers was dead at the scene. Smith would die later that night at an area hospital. The hour delay in calling police may have cost Smith her life.

"The police drove me to the hospital," Norman Smith said. "But it was too late. A doctor asked me to identify her body." Life does not get much worse than that.

Like in Indianapolis, only a very small amount of money was taken. Police eventually located the witness, who provided them with the first sketch of the I-70 killer: a slightly built red haired man, around five foot seven, 150 pounds, stubble for a beard, wearing a brown jacket with an "Uzi" style gun. The witness told police he did not see the suspect escape or see an escape vehicle. The phantom killer again disappeared from sight, this time into the dark of the early Wichita night.

"Initially it was a pretty shocking crime scene," Relph said. "It just did not look like a typical robbery gone bad.

Once we eliminated friends and family, we knew early on it was something very, very different. But who could have predicted this?"

For Tim Relph, the hunt for the I-70 serial killer will never end. He is both hopeful and confident of a solution, even though there have been no new leads in the case since the murders. And like Indianapolis, Wichita has seen a spike in murders. The cases keep piling up on Relph's desk. But with a homicide clearance rate of around 85%, Tim Relph is not a man who gives up easily.

And for Relph, it is still location, location, location. "There seems to be some motivation for him to travel that may possibly be linked beyond the murders. I think there is something driving him to those specific locations. I think there is likely a critical event in 1992 driving him to kill, but I do not think even he knew when he was going to kill next. I think it is going to be events in his life that drove him to this point."

❧

Patricia Magers was 32. The Magers had just purchased the La Bride d'Elegance store the year before. "This was her dream, to own this wedding store, to be independent and self-reliant, and do something she loved," Mark Magers said. "She was one of the most loving people I have ever met. She was just so outgoing. Countless women have stopped me, sometimes at a store or coffee shop, when they realize who I am. They say 'she helped me with my wedding.' Then they tear up and I tear up. There is hardly a week goes by that somebody does not ask me about it."

For Magers, the tears have never stopped. "You see horrible things like this on the news all the time, and although your heart goes out to those people, deep down inside you think 'that will never happen to me.' But obviously none of us are impervious to these things, and it did happen to me. It is still extremely hard for me to comprehend all of this. It is just really hard for me to process. It is just shock and awe."

The pathologist who worked the crime scene said it was the toughest autopsy he ever had to conduct. He not only knew Patricia Magers, he served as the surrogate father at her wedding. Now, nearly 30 years after the crime, Mark Magers states the obvious: Not a single day goes by that he does not think about what happened to the love of his life. "Patricia and I had a very strong marriage. We were just two peas in the same pod. We never did anything that we were not doing together. I was blessed to have met her in the first place."

Magers and I stopped and looked at all the cars driving quickly past the busy area. "There are so many stores in Wichita along the major arteries," he said, then paused before adding, "How he picked this one is anybody's guess."

We stood and looked at each other quietly. Two strangers brought together by a devastating moment decades long gone. I saw the tears well up in Magers' eyes as he spoke slowly. "This heinous crime happened to the one person I loved most on the face of the earth."

ᘓ

I desperately searched to find a friend of Patricia Smith's, from 30 years ago, and finally found one who agreed to meet me.

"You must be Ruth," I said as a woman approached me and Magers.

"I am," she said. "Thank you for finding me."

Ruth Feather was much more than a close friend of Smith's. She still carries Smith's funeral memorial card in her purse, nearly 30 years later.

"She was a fantastic person. She was awesome. I loved her to pieces." Feather looked around, and remembered what life used to be like at the strip mall. And she also cannot forget that night. "I try to always avoid this place because it just brings back too many horrific, terrible memories. I had the news on the television that night and we heard about what happened at the bridal store. I knew I had to get a hold of Patricia's parents. We would cry and cry. We would get angry. We would get frustrated. How can someone just walk in and shoot two women for absolutely no reason? What are you so bitter about in your life that you have to take your frustrations out on two innocent people? When you say horrible, that is an understatement. It was the most devastating, tragic, senseless thing I have ever gone through. And I am still angry about it."

Mark Magers would reopen the bridal shop shortly after the murders but sold it a few months later. Today, Ascent Computer Technology sits in the building.

℀

Norman Smith says his grieving never stopped. "They always say there are five [stages] of grief. Not for me. For me, there were no stages. It was all at once." Smith paused. Then, "In my case, there was no such thing as bargaining."

Smith moved away from Wichita, remarried, and has children from his second marriage. "But it doesn't make up for her loss," he said.

As I prepared to leave, I thanked Magers and Feather for meeting me and enduring a difficult day. We said goodbye and wished each other well. And as I got in my car and began to pull away, I looked back. Magers and Feather, tied to different victims, had never met until today. I watched and waited a few minutes before leaving the parking lot. I saw the two laughing and hugging. I imagined there were tears to follow. I pulled away thinking that what began as a difficult day for them, had somehow ended with smiles and grace. And I smiled too.

CHAPTER 3
"It is like standing in front of a mountain and wondering how you are going to get to the top..."

Michael "Mick" McCown's back had been flaring up for quite some time, and he had a chiropractor appointment on the morning of April 27. When he returned home afterwards, he still did not feel well. He considered taking the rest of the day off and not opening Sylvia's Ceramics Shop, in a busy area of Terre Haute, named after his mother. But he eventually decided to go in. That decision would cost him his life.

Mick McCown was 40 years old. He was an accomplished musician, playing in numerous bands in the Wabash Valley area, specializing in his favorite: the harmonica. The ceramic shop had been a staple in the area since 1969, sitting along a very busy stretch of Highway

41, the main north-south thoroughfare in Terre Haute. It was just blocks north of Interstate 70.

Sometime just after 4pm, a serial killer walked into the store, fatally shot Mick point blank four inches from the back of his head, and fled. Like the other locations, nobody heard or saw a thing. Less than $50 was taken from the store, money was still left in the cash register, and money was still in McCown's pocket, although his wallet was missing.

"We can't say for sure that the wallet was stolen," said longtime Terre Haute Detective Brad Rumsey. "But it was not on McCown's body, or with his family, or at his residence. I would certainly make the assumption his wallet was stolen." When detectives hit the streets, it was eerie how deafening the silence was. Not a witness to anything unusual anywhere in sight. Nothing from the antique store. Nothing from the auto repair shop. The killer snuck in, and snuck out, as always.

Rumsey has held watch on the McCown case since 2019. It was always in his blood. A Terre Haute lad, he attended Indiana State University, majoring in criminology. He has served the police department as a patrolman, detective, field training officer, and hostage negotiator. Prior to that, he served his country in the U.S. Navy and then the National Guard. Retirement is calling Rumsey, but there is still a case he desperately wants to solve.

We arrived in Terre Haute to see a new police station. I asked Rumsey what life was like back in 1992 when a serial killer swept through town.

"We were still writing paper reports here in 1992." He laughed. "Computers are leaps and bounds ahead of where we were in 1992."

Rumsey is the kind of man you could sit and talk to for hours. Easy to chat with and friendly, less guarded than most detectives, but clearly up to speed on dealing with the media. He knew I had made the trip to talk about the serial killer.

In Terre Haute, like Indianapolis and Wichita, the killer was in and out in minutes, onto his next destination: St. Charles. I asked Rumsey why he thought the killer would pick such a busy location in the middle of the day. And why would he steal McCown's wallet and then leave money in his pocket, as well as in the cash register? Like at the other locations, nothing seemed to make any sense.

"Everything about this case certainly does strike me as odd," said Rumsey. "This guy obviously did more than one killing, and at all of the killings, we are dealing with odd times and odd locations. When you consider the times of the day, they are times when people are out and about, busily going back and forth. I think his quirk is he got off on the fact that people were basically right there, right smack in front of him, and he was doing something that heinous and still getting away with it. It probably really got the juices flowing for him knowing that people were right next door or right in front of the place where he was doing these incredibly horrible crimes."

We drove to where Sylvia's Ceramics stood 30 years ago. Rumsey and I looked around the area by the strip mall. And just like the other homicide locations, the question of a getaway vehicle has never been answered. It certainly was not waiting for him in the small parking lot. "After all these years, it is still just a guessing game as far as what was happening with the vehicle," lamented Rumsey, who was serving in the Navy at the time of the McCown murder, repairing flight gear and equipment for F-14 fighter aircrafts. "Clearly this guy did not have a vehicle parked anywhere close by that anybody ever saw. He had to have walked on foot to these places."

"Who kills somebody without a way out?" I asked, bewildered

Rumsey shook his head again. "And yet he is traveling great distances on the interstate, just going back and forth. It just does not make any sense. Like the other killings, the serial killer simply vanished from plain sight. Nobody saw anything. At this point it is still a guessing game. But he had to have walked on foot to these places from somewhere nearby. And that is where his ride must have been waiting for him."

And there was something else very much odd about the Terre Haute killing. The victim was a male. And he was not lured or dragged to the back of the store like the others. McCown's body was found near the front of the store, slumped on the floor, his hand just inches from a ceramic item he had bent down to remove from the shelf, surely at the killer's request. McCown was slightly built, had long hair and an earring. Had the killer mistaken him from a distance for a woman? Perhaps the name "Sylvia's" on the front of the store led him to this location? Did it mean the killer did not stake out the store ahead of time and simply walked in cold?

Rumsey believes the killer was stunned to find out his target was a man, and not a woman like the others. "When you consider all of the other victims are females, and with the store being named Sylvia's, he probably assumed there was a female in there at that time. But yes, it is odd knowing it was a male, and everyone else was a female. McCown may have appeared from behind to be a female to the killer, so I can certainly see how he could have mistaken him for a female. Then you consider that McCown was found on the retail sales floor, in the front of the store, where the other victims were corralled to the back of the store. He may have done that because once he realized he was dealing with a male, he might have thought that 'this guy might wind up fighting me. This guy might not let me walk him to the back of the store like he had planned.' He may have shot him right then and there, as soon as he realized he was dealing with a male, to keep that from happening."

Rumsey has pored over the case file hundreds of times. "The detectives interviewed a lot of people. But no real information was gained from the scene. Detectives really did not gain any steam at all. It was honestly a cold case very early on."

I had reached out to McCown's two sisters, Teresa and Cynthia, to see if they could meet me at the scene. Both agreed, but warned me it might be a difficult day. Returning to where their mother's store was would not only be difficult for both of them, but they had grown distant from each other over the years. Their reunion would not be easy. When our crew arrived to meet them, they talked to me separately, eyeing each other from a distance.

Teresa Lee says neither she nor anybody else in her family believes the killer mistook her brother for a woman. "I do not think that is true," Lee said. "And neither do his friends or the rest of the family. I think whoever killed him went into the ceramics shop because it was named Sylvia's. The killer was expecting a woman to be inside there. The killer was stunned when he found out it was Mick."

Cynthia Brock no longer lived in the area. She got up in the middle of the night and drove hours from her home to meet me. She says she remembers the day of Mick's murder like it was yesterday. She has never spoken about the case since it happened, and it was obvious that it was difficult for her to do so now. "I was watching the evening news that night on television. I remember the reporter came on the screen and said, 'there has been a male body found inside Sylvia's Ceramics store.' I remember I just started screaming and screaming and screaming."

Brock rushed to the scene, where she found her mother had already arrived. "She looked at me like her whole world had just ended, and she was screaming, 'they shot him in the back of the head.' I remember throwing my purse to the ground and then I started screaming [too]."

Brock remembers returning home later that night to help care for her grandfather, who was suffering severely from Alzheimer's Disease. "My grandfather, he could not remember anything for a very long time. But that night he saw the news on the television, and he saw what happened to Mick. And he remembered. We had to find a doctor somewhere and get my grandfather tranquilizers. He did not know anything for all those years, but he suddenly knew all about Mick being murdered."

With that, Cynthia could no longer continue. I walked back over to Teresa. She also remembers that fateful day nearly 30 years ago. "A friend called me. I could tell she was worried. She said, 'have you talked to your mom lately?' I said, 'no, why?' She was very upset. She asked what the name of our family store was, and I said Sylvia's. She said, 'I am sorry, Teresa, but I can't tell you.' I begged her to tell me. She said somebody got hurt at the store. I thought maybe there was an accident, maybe a car accidentally drove into the store. It had happened one time before. I tried calling my family, but I could not get a hold of anybody. I called the store. I still remember their phone number. They said, 'who is this?' I said, 'this is his sister.' They handed the phone to someone else, and they just said he was dead. I fell on the floor screaming. It was just terrible."

Brock remembers the police investigation immediately after Mick was murdered was not very enjoyable for her family, or people who knew Mick. "Once they did not have any clues or suspects, they accused all of us, like we were the ones who did it. But I understand they were just doing their job. The bad guy is usually a family member or knows the victim in some way. In a way it was almost a relief when we heard about a serial killer out there, because that meant the police would quit questioning all of us. None of us wanted Mick killed. He was such a good brother. I want people to know what a good brother he really was. He was my little brother. And he was a wonderfully talented musician."

Teresa said pretty much the same thing. "Everybody loved Mick. The police told us they interviewed all of his friends, and they could not find anybody who did not like Mick. We knew it had to be a stranger."

Rumsey says the hope is now in science. Terre Haute police have recently shipped a new sample of DNA off for testing. "I think the big one in this case is DNA. That is the best way we might be able to identify him. If there is not a DNA match in our Terre Haute case, maybe there will be in another case at one of the other locations. I really do believe that there is going to be a DNA match somewhere to someone. I think there is absolutely a strong chance we can identify this person. Absolutely, I do one hundred percent, yes."

Now, after serving his country and then his community, Rumsey prepares for retirement, knowing his thoughts will never stray very far away from Sylvia's, the McCown family, and the I-70 serial killer. "It is extremely daunting to work a case like this. It is like standing in front of a mountain and wondering how you are going to get to the top," Rumsey said, shaking his head. "There is just so much information to go through. All of the files, all of the years, all of the detectives who have worked so hard to try and solve this case. And unfortunately, a lot of what is in front of you is meaningless, or really of no use to the case. You have to pick out the pieces that really mean something."

Today, Sylvia's Ceramics is a vape shop. Only memories remain of what once was. Mick McCown may have died that day. But not to his family. McCown's father Phillip was so distraught, he stopped driving his own car, and parked it in the garage. He insisted on driving Mick's car instead. And he drove it everywhere, every day. He said it smelled like his son.

And the family turned off the lights at Sylvia's. When it came time to say goodbye, I brought Teresa and Cynthia together, and thanked them for making the effort to meet me. They remarked how they had grown apart over the years, rarely speaking and separated by hundreds of miles. They shared the pain of what happened 30 years ago, and both agreed sometimes it seemed better to just stay away from things. But today they were together, the topic was Mick, and the stories hit both sisters close to home. Today they were smiling and talking. I thought back to watching Mark Magers and Ruth Feather in Wichita. Maybe something good could come from something so terribly bad.

CHAPTER 4
"This guy's motivation was the act of the killing, not the robbery..."

It was 1992, and a quiet spring Sunday afternoon in the newsroom. The Cardinals were playing the Padres on a television in the corner. The day was winding down, the next newscast was looming, and I was already contemplating dinner plans when the phone rang.

"There is a big police scene at the strip mall just off I-70 in St. Charles," the caller said. "There are police cars everywhere. Yellow crime scene tape is up. Looks like something bad."

I quickly started making calls to the police, but got nowhere. The nearby stores were not answering. Something was clearly up. I knew the police routine all too well. Early information would come slowly. But in the middle of an afternoon? At a strip mall? That did not make any sense. Of course, I was not yet aware of a killer who had already struck three other cities.

I grabbed a photographer. "Let's head to St. Charles," I said. "This one just doesn't feel right."

Nancy Christine Kitzmiller was just 24 years old. She grew up in Mustang, Oklahoma, just outside of Oklahoma City, but her family moved to the St. Louis area when she was 10. She had recently graduated from Oklahoma State University with a degree in geography. As with all young people, life was moving very quickly for Nancy. She had recently moved into her own apartment, had interviewed for a cartography job with the Defense Mapping Agency in St. Louis and, most importantly to her, had just bought a Chevy pickup truck days earlier. She had two passions in her life: soccer, and anything and everything to do with the country and western scene. Oklahoma will do that to you.

Nancy did not even begin playing soccer until her senior year of high school, yet incredibly, she waltzed into Stillwater, Oklahoma and wound up becoming the captain of the Oklahoma State women's soccer team in her very first year. And when it came to country and western fare, be it clothes, music, rodeos, horse shows, or her specialty, western dancing, Nancy had few peers. The Texas two-step? She owned the dance floor. With beautiful sparkling blue eyes and long, curly brown hair, she was a friend to everyone, and was still beaming about her family vacation to Paris just a few weeks earlier.

That all would change on May 3, 1992, when the serial killer pulled off Interstate 70 in St. Charles, Missouri, and descended on the Boot Village store where Nancy worked. She was not even supposed to be working that day, but she volunteered to come in so another worker could have the day off. She knew that she would be working alone and opened the store in the Bogey Hills Plaza shopping center, a strip mall just off Interstate 70 at Zumbehl Road, at noon. Around 2:30pm, a customer found Nancy's body in a back room of the store. Like Robin Fuldauer, Patricia Magers, Patricia Smith, and Mick McCown before her, Nancy had been shot point blank in the head, execution style. At first, police detectives believed they were working a robbery gone bad, the type of scene they had worked countless times before. But then they noticed that Nancy's purse had been left behind. And then they discovered that just a small amount of cash was missing from the register. Police scratched their heads. Little money taken, and a woman murdered in broad daylight at a busy store? The scene never made sense.

At the time, Boot Village was nestled between a beauty salon and a veterinary clinic. Detectives began digging into their crime scene. One witness said they saw a man sitting outside the store around 12:30pm. A passerby reported seeing who they thought might be the killer, saying it was a man of medium height with dull red hair. Because detectives first thought they were working a robbery, they focused on another robbery that had occurred a month earlier in the same strip mall. A man with a gun had forced two workers at the Hallmark gift shop into a back room where he sprayed their faces with mace. He stole $200 from the store and fled. The modus operandi looked eerily similar. But now a murder scene over a lesser amount of cash? It did not make any sense.

And where was the suspect? In broad daylight, nobody saw him walk in or walk out of the store. And unlike the other I-70 serial locations, there was no residential area nearby for the killer to park and then walk to a getaway vehicle. Bogey Hills Golf Course sat behind the store, a difficult venue for a killer to navigate on a weekend afternoon full of golfers.

Police were tight lipped at the scene. Usually, they will point the press in the direction of what they think might have happened. But not today. Today was met with heads shaking and looks of bewilderment. I spotted an officer I knew and pulled him to the side.

"What is up?" I asked him.

He just shook his head. "This is a bad one," he said.

"Robbery?" I asked. He shook his head no.

"Rape?" Another no.

"Family? Friend?"

The officer paused for a second. "They don't seem to think so right now."

"Then what?" I asked.

A shrug of the shoulders.

St. Charles police worked the scene furiously, but by day's end, they had very few leads on their hands, and more questions than answers.

My photographer and I headed back to the newsroom. He had covered more homicides than I had. "What do you think?" I asked him.

"I don't know," he said. "Who pulls off the highway, in the middle of a busy Sunday afternoon, walks into a small store, shoots somebody in the head, and then just walks out without taking anything?"

"Nobody," I answered.

"Exactly," he said. "Trust me, something is really different about this one."

Within days, the St. Charles police department knew exactly what was different. Richard Plummer was one of the lead detectives on the case. A homicide veteran, it did not take him long to realize what the police were dealing with. "His motive certainly does not appear to be robbery," Plummer said before pausing. "This guy is going in there to kill."

The Major Case Squad, a group of specialized detectives in the St. Louis area dealing with difficult to solve homicide cases, was activated. Sixteen officers worked the case around the clock. Pat Morici, a St. Louis city homicide detective, would be the lead commander. "It is the only case that I never solved while working with the Major Case Squad. It was horrible not to solve it. Very, very frustrating."

Morici would retire from the police force two years later. "The Kitzmiller case still haunts me to this day," he said.

St. Ann Police Captain John O'Rando would lead the investigators on the scene. "We just had an extreme lack of evidence there," O'Rando said. "At first, you think it is a robbery that somehow went horribly bad, and then you realize it is something completely different. This certainly was not a routine homicide investigation. You look for a motive, and there just never appeared to be one. Nothing made sense. And without a motive, it is a very tough investigation for the detectives."

O'Rando is also retired. Like Morici, he too still follows the case. "Yeah, I still try to follow it. But 30 years is a long time to try to solve a crime. Very difficult, but I hope they can."

Recently retired St. Charles detective Don Stepp held the case in his lap for decades. We made plans to meet and go back to the crime scene at the Bogey Hills plaza. We parked our cars in the busy shopping center parking lot and looked around. "There certainly would have been a very large number of people here that day," Stepp said. "Especially at that time. It certainly would not have been my choice of a murder location. I feel like his guy was very, very calculated. I do not think he just walked in on the spur of the moment to murder someone. I think he looked at what he had in front of him. I think he analyzed it very thoroughly."

Stepp and I walked around the area. "How could he have gotten away unnoticed?" I asked.

Stepp paused for the question that could not be answered, then said, "It is possible he could have gotten away out the back way, by the golf course. But he did not. He came in right through the front door and walked out right through the front door. Right into a busy group of people in the middle of a Sunday afternoon. If we had that vehicle of his, or his mode of transportation, that would be a very big missing piece in this puzzle. I do not believe he was in any of these scenes very long. He knew he was risking way too much if he did. Wichita showed that." Stepp paused again. "But Wichita did not scare him. And it did not stop him."

And as puzzling as the leads were as the years and decades moved on, St. Charles detectives did have some suspects. In 1994, police arrested Lonnie Wiseman, a career criminal, in Idaho. They questioned him about the I-70 murders, only to discover that he was sitting in prison at that time. Wiseman was not a free man forever, though. He was charged in 2013 for a 1994 murder in Virginia. That case was solved, nearly 20 years later, using new DNA evidence. In 1995, detectives traveled to Dallas to interview a suspect in prison, but that fizzled. In 1996, police went so far as to call a news conference, where they named Robert Craig Cox as a suspect. Cox was also sitting in a Texas Prison at the time of the murder, with a rap sheet that included robbery, assault, rape, kidnapping, and murder. He admitted in interviews to a fascination with notorious serial killer Ted Bundy. But those dots never connected. Today, Cox still sits behind bars. And In 2001, the FBI questioned an Indiana truck driver named Randall Bishop. He matched the composite sketch, police were intrigued that he was a truck driver, and he was facing a rape charge at the time. But DNA in that investigation did not match up with the I-70 scenes.

Detectives would work alongside the FBI lab in Quantico, Virginia to form a profile on the I-70 killer. They went through the process twice. Both times, results suggested the killer was likely from the Indianapolis area, and that he was likely fulfilling some sort of fantasy.

Through it all, there sat Don Stepp. "I never once thought I was going to be a police officer. It is something that never crossed my mind whatsoever. When I was 18 years old, right after high school, I joined the United States Marine Corps. When I got out of the Marines, I wanted something like I had there. I wanted teamwork, I wanted camaraderie. I wanted to be part of something important."

What he got was a 30-year cold case. "When I was assigned to the Nancy Kitzmiller case it was not just the folder on my desk. It was the closet full of folders. There were piles and piles of documents, and all of the work that went into the original investigation by different detectives before me. It was very overwhelming to look at to say the least."

Stepp went to work, first trying to build a relationship with Nancy's parents, Don and Carol Kitzmiller. And for her parents, there is never an easy day. And while they appreciate the work of the task force, their desire is to be removed from the limelight as much as possible. "Every single day, you think about her," Carol Kitzmiller said. "It is horrible how much I miss her. It is important that this man be caught, not just for us, but for all the other families too."

"You look at this case," Don Kitzmiller says, "and there is someone outside of society who just walks in at random and does this. We talk and we pray every day. We keep our fingers crossed that the police will catch this person. There is not much else that we can do."

For the parents, there is heartbreak. Still today, they avoid the Zumbehl Road exit off Highway 70. When they have errands to run, they go someplace other than the Bogey Hills Plaza.

For Stepp, there is only one goal. "There is nothing that would make me happier in my entire life than for me to tell Don and Carol Kitzmiller and their family that we know what happened to Nancy."

And he says they will. "There is not a doubt in my mind that someday we will be able to solve this case," Stepp said. "There will be answers given to the family and the individual who did this to her will be identified and held responsible for these crimes."

Today, the Boot Village store is a Panera Bread. Hundreds of people are coming and going throughout the day. And 30 years can erase a lot of memories. But not for Don Stepp.

We walked up closer to the building. "There is also not a doubt in my mind." Stepp said, "that if you walked in there today and asked everybody what this real estate was infamous for, not a single person would have a clue."

As Stepp left the department, he handed the case over to Detective Kelly Rhodes, who was a mere toddler when the I-70 serial killer swept the country. The Nancy Kitzmiller case will be her sole focus, every day. Rhodes is fully aware of the amount of leg work done before her and relishes the opportunity to work on the daunting task that now lies in front of her. "I was very excited when they asked me to do this," Rhodes says. "The previous investigators have set us up for success and with all the new technology that we have now, I feel like we can bring this case to a close."

Both veteran detectives like Stepp and younger ones like Rhodes agree that a fresh set of eyes can often do wonders for a case, especially a cold one. And Rhodes is ready. "I know this is a very big case, and I feel really good about our ability to solve this. When I look at this case, there does not seem to be any motivation for these crimes. Even the amount of money taken was very minimal, so it does not even appear that robbery was a motive. We have no answers and no reasons why. It is just senseless."

Nancy Kitzmiller was buried back where she was born, in Oklahoma. She had her western boots on, ready to two-step at her next stop.

CHAPTER 5
"I said, 'where did this guy go?'"

Sarah Blessing rolled out of her bed, helped her children get ready for school, fed her two pets, and prepared her usual breakfast of fresh fruit. She drove to visit her ailing friend, Karen Winney, as she did almost every week. Winney said they talked about heaven and people who had recently passed away.

Sarah pulled into the Woodson Village shopping center in Raytown, Missouri, a suburb of Kansas City, just before noon to open her store. "The Store of Many Colors" was a small health care store sitting on the very end of the strip mall owned and operated by Blessing and five of her friends, selling goods for improving spiritual and physical health. Here you could find items like herbs, crystals, vitamins, clean water machines, and even miniature exercise trampolines. The group had just celebrated a successful grand opening of their store three weeks earlier. To make their schedules work, Sarah and her friends would take turns working at the store. Today was Sarah's turn. She would be alone.

Sarah called her husband Sonny on the phone around 2pm for their usual afternoon chat. They talked about how business was going at the store that day, their two boys at home and, of course, the family dog and cat.

Next door to Sarah's store, Tim Hickman arrived a little early for his evening shift at his video store, Video Attic. It was around 5:30pm. Business was slow on the sunny day, so Hickman had decided to relieve his mother and sister who were working the store together that afternoon.

Around 6:15pm, the owner of an auctioneer store across the plaza from Sarah's store saw a mysterious unidentified man walk in and out of his store. Around the same time, another witness spotted a well-dressed man in a gray sports coat, slacks, and dress shoes walking across the large parking lot and heading toward Blessing's store. A serial killer, unconcerned about being spotted in broad daylight, was about to strike.

Our crew pulled into the Woodson Village Center and I looked around. There was what would have been Sarah's old store on the far end. Next to it would have been Hickman's video store. I looked across the parking lot where the auctioneer store must have been. I looked around and imagined what was happening that day. The mysterious man must have walked right past where I stood on his way toward Sarah's store.

Then I walked over to what would have been Tim Hickman's old store, where we agreed to meet. Hickman arrived and was clearly nervous. He would prove to be the best witness in the case, the one person who came face to face with the murderer and could still recall it like it was yesterday. Hickman was a quiet, reserved man, who wore his feelings on his sleeve. Today, those feelings were on overload. We shared small talk, then I asked Hickman to walk me through that fateful day. He said it began around 6:30pm, when he glanced out his window and looked across the parking lot.

"I just happened to glance up, and I see a gentleman coming across the parking lot. He had on a sports coat, and I thought 'wow that is weird,' because it was a relatively warm night outside, and he was much more well-dressed than most of our customers at the plaza. I kept watching him, and he was walking my way, like he is coming right toward my store. I got distracted doing something, but then I looked up again a few minutes later and he had stepped right in front of my door, like he was looking inside for something, but he did not come in. I looked at him and he looked at me. I think he was a little bit shocked at what he saw, because if he had scoped the store a little bit earlier, my mom and my sister were working here. I just remember he looked around and seemed kind of shocked. He looked at me like, 'huh, that is not what I kind of thought it was.' I looked right at his face. Then he turned, left, and just took off. I just thought it was odd."

Minutes later, the murderer walked a couple of steps, and entered Blessing's store. "About two or three minutes after I see him leave my store, I hear what sounds like a pop," Hickman says. "It sounds to me almost like a gunshot. Then I said, 'no, that can't possibly be it.' Then I hear a door slam. And I have never told anybody this before, but I grabbed my gun from under my counter, a .38, and I had it behind my back. I jumped right through the front door. I took a portable phone with me. I saw Sarah's door was just closing, and the guy I saw earlier looking through my door, right at me, was going around the corner of Sarah's store. His back was to me, and I did not see his face this time, but I could tell it was the same man by his clothes. It was definitely the same guy, absolutely no doubt in my mind, that was looking through my window moments earlier. Same guy, same clothes. He was whipping around the corner of the building fast. I stood there for maybe 20 to 30 more seconds, trying to figure out what was happening. I said to myself, 'something is very wrong here.' I looked both ways, and he was gone, just disappeared, up over the steep hill leading to the road. That is a very steep hill. It could not have been more than 30 or 45 seconds now. I said, 'Where did this guy go?' I ran back to her store and immediately called for Sarah."

Hickman paused when Sarah did not answer. Fearing the worst, Hickman says he looked in through Sarah's window but did not see anything. He finally stepped inside the store and found her lifeless body lying in a pool of blood. "All I could see were her feet sticking out. I immediately called the police. I said 'There has been someone shot here. Please, I need a police officer here immediately.' By the time they arrived, it was just total pandemonium everywhere."

With that, Hickman paused, choking back tears that had been building for nearly 30 years. "I did not know her very well, but she seemed like a very nice young lady. I am sorry. I can't go any further. I am sorry. But even after all these years, it just still bothers me." I gave Hickman space and time. We walked around the plaza.

"Tim, there was nothing you could have done…" I began telling him.

"I know, I know," he said. "Everyone tells me that. I just can't get it out of my mind."

Police would arrive minutes after Hickman called. Sarah Blessing was pronounced dead at the scene. Detectives quickly began canvassing the entire area around Woodson Village Center. They found a grocery store clerk who was gathering shopping carts in the parking lot, and he said he saw the exact same thing Hickman did: a man leaving Blessing's store, heading toward the steep hill behind her store, leading to Woodson Road. They located another witness who reported seeing a similar looking man walking down a nearby busy street around 6:45pm, just minutes after Blessing was murdered.

Sarah Blessing was 37 years old. Only a small amount of cash was missing from her store, similar to the murder scenes in Indianapolis, Wichita, Terre Haute, and St. Charles.

As days and weeks went by, Hickman learned what he did not know on that fateful day. "I thought what happened to Sarah was something random, like maybe he was trying to rob someplace and picked hers instead of mine. Then I heard on the news that it was a serial killer. I did not know anything about an I-70 killer driving up and down the highway killing people across the country. Then the police called me and said they had a composite sketch of the killer from Wichita. Police asked me to come in and look at the picture and compare it to the man I saw." And it did not take Hickman very long. "It was close. Very close. Hair color. Height. Build. Very similar."

I asked Hickman if he thought that, after all these years have passed, he could pick the serial killer out of a police lineup, if the case ever got that far and he ever got that chance. He did not hesitate. "Yes I could. No doubt in my mind."

The Store of Many Colors never reopened after Sarah's death. Sarah's husband Sonny has passed away, never getting the satisfaction of seeing her killer captured. Hickman returned to open his video store the next day. "I went back to open, and there must have been 40 news trucks here. I just kept on driving."

Tim Hickman is still haunted by that day in 1992. He often wonders what might have happened if the killer had struck a little earlier in the day, while his mother and sister were working in their store. And he wonders if he acted fast enough when fate put him in the path of a serial killer. I watched as Hickman had difficulty coming up with the right words. It was all he could do to compose himself. You could tell he had a hard time letting go, even 30 years later. It was heartbreaking.

"You did all you could do, Tim," I said. "Nobody could have done anything more." We shook hands and said goodbye. I watched him get into his car and leave. And I realized, in a much different way, that he was a victim too.

രഃ

Chris Shrout can only shake his head. Due to attrition and cutbacks, the Raytown Police Department has lost many officers over the years. It is all they can do to keep up with the crimes of the day. And now, the I-70 serial killer case, 30 years old, sits on Shrout's young lap. "A lot of those older detectives who first worked on this case are no longer here. Being new to a cold case like this one, you are obviously thinking about things outside of the box. Everybody has a different perspective on things. A lot of it is me tracking down people from 30 years ago. A lot of it is me going through thousands of pages of reports. You are investigating a crime and not a person, and then you have to go and find the person. It can be overwhelming while you are still trying to do your day job." He smiles and shakes his head again. "Actually, it can be very overwhelming."

And Shrout has begun putting those fresh set of eyes on the case. Like everyone else, he has questions about the I-70 killer that seem to have no answers. "It makes me question what brought him a little bit farther out," Shrout wondered. The Raytown scene is about three miles off of Interstate 70, not as close to the highway as the other murder scenes. "Was it because he was more comfortable, and maybe knew the area a little bit? Is it possible that he knew somebody here?"

The Raytown case also had another oddity, different from the other locations. The killer, although only in Blessing's store for a few minutes, rummaged through her belongings. "I do not know," Shrout wondered again, seeking answers he knew he might never find. "Maybe he was just getting a little more brave."

Shrout and I just shook our heads. And then we looked over to the steep hill behind Blessing's store, where Hickman saw the killer flee. It did not make sense for a getaway path. "Maybe one of us should try running up that hill," I suggested with a smile. "You know, see how long it takes, and how hard it was for the killer."

Shrout laughed. He knew I was not volunteering, and besides, he had already beaten me to it. "I decided to run up that hill myself," Shrout said. "I wanted to see for myself what it was like."

"And?" I asked.

He shook his head again. "I can tell you, you do not want to be running up that hill."

CHAPTER 6
"This is a totally different animal than anything we normally have to deal with..."

Roger Spurgeon, David Ellison, and Columbus Ricks could only shake their heads in amazement and imagine what was happening at their Indianapolis Police Department 30 years ago, when the phone call came from Wichita telling them that the same gun that was used to kill Patricia Magers and Patricia Smith was used to kill Robin Ruldauer just days earlier.

"I am pretty sure it had to be very stunning to the early investigators," Spurgeon said, "to find out that there was a positive link between the two cases in Indianapolis and Wichita just days apart. They were so far apart from each other distance-wise, but yet so close in time to each other. When they did realize that they had a random serial killer on their hands, it must have been like 'this is a totally different animal than anything we normally have to deal with.' We certainly have not had too many people traveling across the country doing random homicides every couple of days."

Spurgeon paused and looked at the Batteries Plus store, the building that used to be the Payless Shoes store where Robin Fuldauer was the first victim of the I-70 serial killer. "And we certainly have not had too many people traveling across the country doing homicides without a motive. That is what the early investigators had to deal with. Where do you even get started?" So far away, so quick between killings, and no motive. It was no longer an investigation of family and friends.

In reality, there were very few suspects once police realized what they were dealing with after Indianapolis and Wichita. Just a crazed madman on the loose traveling quickly across the country. There was no chapter in the homicide book dealing with serial killers who strike days later and hundreds of miles apart across the country seemingly without a motive. Detectives began scrambling. Quickly, they asked themselves the obvious question about the elephant in the room: What if Indianapolis was not the first stop on the killer's spree? They began calling around to numerous police departments to see what might be on their books, but found nothing. In the meantime, the phones began ringing, and the tips began coming in, but not exactly what the detectives were hoping for. "We would get calls from disgruntled wives," Ellison lamented. "They would tell us to investigate their husbands. It would be comical if it was not true."

The tips went nowhere fast.

Mike Crooke went back over his early notes on the Fuldauer case. "For detectives, and police departments, there is no way in the world you are planning on something like this. No way. It just shocks you. We must have had about 30 people working on the Fuldauer case nonstop. As you can imagine, none of the investigators had ever gone through something like this before, certainly not with the distances this guy traveled."

Crooke says one of the first questions was the vehicle involved. "Hitchhiking was the original thought, and I still can't completely disregard that possibility. I have also thought about him having a vehicle parked somewhere, maybe along the highway to get out of town quickly. But that would have been awfully risky for him. Police could have come by and they surely would have towed the vehicle away."

Crooke remembers those early days of the investigation, the lack of suspects, and the frustrations for the detectives. "We literally went through and got hotel registrations from every single hotel across Interstate 70, up and down the highway all over. We checked out toll booths, we checked out license plates, we looked at every traffic stop. At one point I know we had 67,000 names in a computer database. And we checked out every single one of those

67,000." And none of them panned out. The phantom killer had disappeared into thin air, without leaving a trace behind.

Some detectives thought the killer must have been an over the road truck driver to make that long haul trip and kill again so quickly in Wichita. But where was his big rig? It certainly was not parked in front of any strip mall to be used as a getaway vehicle. It likely was not sitting unattended along the highway. The phantom killer appeared and disappeared into thin air.

After Wichita, police quickly realized their first hunches were incorrect. They were no longer looking for a homeless man as a suspect, and likely not a hitchhiker who would risk bringing someone else along for the ride into his insane world. And with the ballistics in Wichita now matching those in Indianapolis, police could also rule out family members and acquaintances as potential suspects. Early in the case, detectives only had one thing to go on: Without any recent or similar killings nearby, were there any other cases, perish the thought, of serial killers in their midst?

An early lead in the case came not from Indianapolis or Wichita, but from Dyersburg, Tennessee, where, just a little over a month before the 1-70 killing spree began, Donald Waterhouse shot and killed his parents inside their home. That might not seem like much of a connection, but as police followed hundreds of leads, it was soon apparent that Waterhouse bore a striking resemblance to

the composite sketch police had from Wichita, and like
the I-70 victims, he shot them in the head with a .22
caliber weapon. After shooting his parents, Waterhouse
fled Tennessee and headed north. His truck was later
found abandoned in East St. Louis, right off I-70, placing
him in the Midwest during the time of the killings. He
would not be captured until October, six months after the
I-70 murders stopped, Investigators in Indiana, Kansas,
Missouri, and Tennessee all began trading information on
Waterhouse, and the FBI hit the streets in Dyersburg. But
Waterhouse would later be cleared of the I-70 murders.

Detectives then began calling around the country
searching for other possible serial killer cases that might
be on the books. They found a man named Neal Falls,
who had been pulled over by police in 20 states while he
traveled the country doing his ill will. In the spring of
1992, Falls was living in Greensburg, Kansas, only about
100 miles west of Wichita. Police discovered he was
obsessed with military paraphernalia, and he also matched
the early composite sketch. Police would question him
about the I-70 murders but had no physical evidence to
connect him. Falls' good fortune would not last long,
however. He would later be killed during a struggle with
a prostitute after holding her at gunpoint. After his death,
police searched his car and found bulletproof vests, a
machete, plastic trash bags, axes, a shovel, knives, bleach,
and a sledgehammer. They were able to link those items to
the unsolved murders and disappearances of nine women

in three states, including Illinois. But they could not tie Falls to anything from the I-70 murders.

Then there was a man named Donald Blom. He also matched the early composite sketch, owned a .22 semi caliber weapon, and had a long rap sheet. In 1975, Blom was convicted of kidnapping and raping a 14-year-old girl. He was sentenced to 40 years in prison, but only served three. After numerous run-ins with the law, in 1992, the year of the I-70 killings, a psychologist warned that Blom had the propensity for "potentially devastating results" if he was not supervised by a mental health professional. Sure enough, in 2000, Blom was convicted of murdering a 19-year-old girl in Minnesota. Police have always suspected he was a serial killer, but there was never any evidence to connect him to the I-70 killings. Blom would later die in prison of natural causes.

But when it came time to look for serial killers, Indianapolis police detectives did not have to look very far. After all, this is where Herb Baumeister called home. Born in 1947, Herbert Richard Baumeister struggled from the very beginning. He was diagnosed with schizophrenia as a teenager. Friends recall him playing with dead animals and then bringing them to school. He would attend Indiana University but soon drop out. His father then had him committed to a mental institution. When Baumeister was released, he landed a job at the Indianapolis Star newspaper, and then later at the Indiana Bureau of Motor Vehicles. But that later job ended abruptly when it was discovered that Baumeister had urinated on a letter that was to be sent to the governor of Indiana. Friends thought it was strange that Baumeister drove a hearse.

Baumeister would marry a woman named Julie and they would have three children. Determined to start anew, Baumeister would borrow money from his mother and open a Sav-A-Lot grocery store. Business soon boomed, and he opened a second store. Herb Baumeister, the schizophrenic who wound up in a mental institution, the man who urinated on a letter that was to be sent to the governor of the state, was not only on his way to becoming a millionaire, he became an important person in the Indianapolis community. Baumeister then purchased Fox Hollow Farm, a beautiful setting resting on 18 acres of wooded land in Westfield, Indiana, about 30 miles north of Indianapolis. He lived in an 11,000-square-foot Tudor style mansion with all the luxuries man could buy, from an indoor swimming pool to a horse riding stable. Herb Baumeister was living the rags to riches American Dream.

Except the American Dream was really a national nightmare. The strait-laced husband, father, businessman, and community icon was living a double life, one that was laced with blood and body parts scattered across the Midwest.

Whenever his wife was out of town, Baumeister would frequent gay bars in the Indianapolis area, going by the name of Brian Smart. He would then bring men back to Fox Hollow Farm to show them his mansion. By the early 1990s, multiple gay men began disappearing in the Indianapolis area. They seemed to have similar age, height, and weight patterns. Detectives working the disappearances then got a tip claiming that a gay bar patron calling himself Brian Smart had killed a man. They were given a license plate number and traced Brian Smart back to Herb Baumeister. Investigators quickly went to search his home, but Baumeister was not there, and Julie denied them access to the property. But Julie Baumeister would soon become suspicious when one of the Baumeister children found a human skull while playing in the woods of Fox Hollow Farms. Julie went to the woods to look around, and found another pile of human bones. When she questioned Herb about it, he claimed it was a medical skeleton device that his father, a doctor, had given him years ago when Herb was a child.

Things soon began to unravel for Baumeister. The Save-A-Lot business that was booming soon started to suffer, and with it so did the Baumeister finances and marriage. Herb and Juie began arguing. And now, Julie had begun to wonder. When her husband went out of town on a business trip, she decided to call the police back. She told them they could now come and search Fox Hollow Farm. Police arrived quickly, and the search did not take long. Within days, more than 10,000 bone fragments were found in the land around the mansion. Incredibly, bones and body parts that were barely covered with leaves sat just 50 feet behind the Baumeister home.

Eleven male bodies were uncovered by forensic experts. And, as the years went by, and ownership of Fox Hollow Farm changed hands, more body parts were found. Many of the victims have never been identified. Indianapolis police would call their search "a mass disaster scene."

Besides those bodies on his estate, Baumeister is suspected in the killing deaths of at least nine more men whose bodies were found along Interstate 70 between Indiana and Ohio, starting in the Indianapolis area and heading east. Julie Baumeister told police that her husband made hundreds of business trips from Indianapolis to Ohio, always using Interstate 70. In all, authorities now say Herb Baumeister may be tied to nearly 30 murders around the Midwest.

To detectives, you had a serial killer, in the early '90s, starting in Indianapolis, with numerous bodies strewn along Interstate 70. It was enough to pique the interest of investigators in the Fuldauer case, even with the different sexes of the victims, and the fact that the I-70 killings had no sexual motive. After all, how many known serial killers were living in the area at the time?

Herb Baumeister was slightly taller than the composite sketch of the serial killer, but the weight may have matched, as might his light hair and his boyish face. But there was no suspect to search for. With police now clearly on his murderous tail, Baumeister packed his bags and fled to Canada. He left behind a three-page suicide note saying how sorry he was about his marriage and his business, but made no mention of the eleven bodies found on his land, or the others found along Interstate 70 that all appeared to lead to him. His note said he was going to eat a peanut butter sandwich and then go to sleep.

When police located his car at Pinery Provincial Park on Lake Huron eight days after he disappeared. He had already put a .357 Magnum to his forehead and pulled the trigger. Herb Baumeister would take his place as the most prolific serial killer in Indiana history.

For a while, Fox Hollow Farm was a tourist attraction, where for $90 visitors got a seven-hour ghost hunt, and could see the Tudor style mansion, the indoor pool, and the riding stable. Then they were able to tour the woods where the multiple murders occurred, and see the exact sites where body parts were discovered. After that, there were refreshments to be had and souvenirs to be purchased. The tour sold out weeks in advance.

What better place to visit on a fall day, I thought. So our crew left Indianapolis and drove north to Westfield. Fences parallel the road that enters the land. You can see the horse stables on one side of the mansion. The woods around the property where the bodies were found were turning barren with the upcoming winter weather. On this day, the entrance was closed and construction was going on. I really was not in the mood for body parts and ghosts anyway.

CHAPTER 7
"I just played cat and mouse too long with the police and they finally figured it out…"

Tim Relph is chasing the I-70 serial killer now. But back in the day...

It was a cold January morning in 1974. Relph was a seventh grader, one of eight children in the house. And he vividly remembers the day a family of four was murdered down the street from his home, and how terribly frightened he was. Each day on his way to school, his path took him past the Otero family home. Tim Relph did his best not to look.

Dennis Rader went to the Otero home on that January night just after 7pm. He had cut the phone lines behind the house and stood in the cold, dark night waiting for a way in. When one of the Otero children opened the door to let the family dog out, Dennis Rader walked right through that door, pulled out a gun, and ordered the family into a back bedroom. He then tied all of them up.

"I realized that, you know, I did not have a mask on or anything," Rader later admitted in court. "So they had already ID'd me. And I made the decision to go ahead to put 'em down, I guess, strangle them." Rader says it was not what he had planned, but was just a spur of the moment decision. He strangled the father, Joseph, first, then the mother, Julie. Rader made the children sit in the same room and recalled them watching and screaming. Rader would then strangle nine-year-old Joey Otero, leaving only eleven-year-old Josephine still alive. "I then took her to the basement and eventually hung her," Rader testified, showing no emotion or remorse.

や

December 2021. My team pulled into Wichita late at night. Relph said he would meet with me, but I thought we might have to put it off until the next day. "No, no, come on over," Relph said. "I will meet you at the department."

When we arrived, Relph looked tired. "Worked all day yesterday," he said. "Went home, then had a double homicide. Worked that all through the night. Then again all day today."

I told Relph this could wait. "No way, brother," he said. "You came all this way. We have got a serial killer to try to catch."

Relph was the detective I was most interested in meeting. After all, he had done it before. And he did it to the man who haunted him in his dreams.

"You have gone down this road once before," I said to Relph. He nodded and gave me a tired smile. There may be science, technology, and DNA to help police solve cases like the I-70 killer. But at the end of the day, you had better have a Tim Relph on your side too. He is dogged in his pursuit, never giving up on a clue or a case. I told him I assumed that to solve a case like this, you needed both science and good old fashioned police work.

"You got that right, brother." He smiled.

From 1974 until 1991, Dennis Rader would murder 10 people in Wichita. And into his world stepped Tim Relph.

I asked Relph to take me back. "Several years ago, I was involved in a case we solved that was 30 years old," Relph said, his voice trailing off. He paused and I waited. Then he continued, "So, I know it can happen."

Relph is focused on the I-70 serial killer now. But he can't help but think back to the madman who became known as the BTK killer in Relph's hometown. Dennis Rader grew up in the small town of Pittsburg, Kansas. He spent four years in the Air Force, where he served as a mechanic, then landed a job at the Cessna Aircraft Company in Wichita. He married Paula Dietz and they had two children. The family lived in a three-bedroom ranch house in the quiet suburb of Park City, just north of Wichita. Rader was a boy scout leader and served as president of his church, Christ Lutheran.

Dennis Rader was the typical neighbor next door. Except he wasn't. He would soon become known as "BTK." Bind. Torture. Kill. Like the I-70 killer, Rader developed his own unique pattern. It began on that January night with the Otero family. Taunting the police, and feeding his own need for publicity, Rader then left a note detailing the murders, describing the gruesome scenes, and announcing his intentions to kill again. But instead of sending the note to the police, he sent it to the Wichita Eagle newspaper, told them to go to the Wichita public library, and instructed them to find the most recent copy of Applied Engineering Mechanics. There, inside, he left an envelope with all the details of the murder.

When the story hit the papers, complete with Rader's promises to kill again, Wichita was in a panic. And it stayed that way for 17 years as Rader played cat and mouse with police, keeping Wichita on edge.

Rader was not just killing. He was enjoying it. He was playing a game of catch me if you can with the Wichita Police Department. And Tim Relph was about to deal with his childhood demons head on.

And thus began nearly two decades of terror for the city of Wichita. Whereas the I-70 serial killer shot his victims in the back of the head, Dennis Rader's preferred method of murder was strangulation. But he was hardly a professional. Sometimes he failed to finish the job, and his victims would regain consciousness. When they did, Rader would whisper in their ears that he was "BTK." Then he would make sure they were dead. It left police to wonder if his initial failures were intentional.

"That was his own personal form of torture," said Relph. "His signature. His calling card. He certainly wanted them to know that they were not just being killed, but they were being killed by BTK, like it was some sort of honor."

Rader's final victim was a woman named Dolores Davis, who was retired and living alone. There was no messing around this time waiting in the cold, dark night for a way to get into her house. Rader simply threw a cinder block through her front window. "She came out of the bedroom and thought a car had crashed into her house," Rader testified. "I told her that I was wanted by the police and I was on the run. I handcuffed her and talked to her. I calmed her down."

Things looked good for Delores for a few minutes. "Then I removed her handcuffs, tied her up, and strangled her," Rader said nonchalantly. "Then I dumped her body under a bridge," he concluded.

While Rader was on his murderous spree, Relph was pursuing a career as a police officer. He graduated as the top cadet in his class. He would work hundreds of homicide cases. When the BTK killer went silent for years, many thought he was dead. But Relph would not let it go, and threw himself into another look at the case.

And then, Dennis Rader became bored. He needed to seek the limelight again, and he decided to return to kill. It was 2005, more than 30 years after his first murder, and 14 years after his last. Dennis Rader had long disappeared from the headlines. Wichita felt safe again. And then suddenly, out of nowhere, Dennis Rader began sending letters to both the Wichita Eagle and KAKE-TV. Once, he told them where he had left a cereal box on the side of an old country road. "Cereal boxes because I am a serial killer," Rader wrote. Inside the box, Rader would announce his return by dressing up small dolls and putting his victims' names on them. He was so confident he could outsmart the police that he enrolled at Wichita State University and took classes in, of course, law enforcement. And to rub it in, after he lost his job at Cessna Aircraft, Rader went to work for ADT security systems, where business was booming as so many Wichita families had ordered the security systems in hopes of protecting themselves from the BTK killer.

While Dennis Rader was no longer murdering, he was laughing at police detectives, which now included a young and recently promoted detective named Tim Relph. And then Rader, still feeding his ego and enjoying seeing his name in the newspaper, made his mistake. He put another cereal box in a Home Depot employee's truck. Inside was a letter to the police department, saying he was tired of dealing with the newspapers, and he wanted to use the new technology of a floppy disk to communicate with police.

He asked them if they had the ability to trace a floppy disk if he mailed it to them. Apparently Rader assumed that the Wichita Police Department, after decades of picking up bodies thanks to Rader, was behind the times and that they would tell him the truth.

"Now be honest," Rader asked in his letter. He then told them to respond to him by writing to a man named Rex, in the newspaper's classified ads, a la Madonna in "Desperately Seeking Susan." The Wichita Police Department obliged, hedging the truth just a tad. "We wrote back into the classified ads and said, 'Rex, it will be OK,'" Relph remembered, a sly smile on his face.

Then, incredibly, Rader mailed police the floppy disk. The police department took it to forensics, and the disk's data was immediately traced to Christ Lutheran Church. That stunned detectives. Their suspect was involved with the church? They began checking all of the church's files, and eventually traced the disk to a church user named Dennis. They went through the church registry and there was only one Dennis, Dennis Rader who lived in nearby Park City.

Police were stunned. After all the years of murders, followed by years of silence, they had a name and an address. And then suddenly they had more. They discovered surveillance video showing a man driving a black Jeep Cherokee and dropping what clearly appeared to be another BTK package into a truck. Tim Relph did not need an invitation. He got in his car and headed north to Park City. Relph drove to Rader's house. And there, in the driveway, sat a black Jeep Cherokee.

Police moved quickly, calling in some 200 officers, along with helicopters and a tank. They stood standby in the area and watched as Rader left for work. Tim Relph followed in his car. Police surrounded his workplace, then apprehended Rader as he went on his lunch break. They loaded him into a squad car and took him to the police department. Behind the wheel was Tim Relph.

I asked him what that moment must have felt like, and all he could do was shake his head. The demons were flying away. The child who grew up fearful of Rader played a crucial role in taking a serial killer off the street.

Dennis Rader would wind up confessing to 10 Wichita murders and receive consecutive life sentences that amounted to 175 years in jail without the possibility of parole. When he was finally caught, the media-starved Rader stated the obvious. "I just played cat and mouse too long with the police and they finally figured it out." Rader emphasized "finally." After all, he was still the smartest man in the room, except for that floppy disk.

I asked Relph why he thought Rader played the back and forth game with not just the media, but the police. He could only smile as he reflected on the days he chased his first serial killer. "Most people do not do what Dennis Rader did. Most people do not try to communicate with police. Trying to exchange communication with the police department is a very dangerous game." And now Relph's late night, tired smile was very wide. The implication was clear. Dennis Rader thought he was smarter than the Wichita Police Department. He was not.

Police apparently captured Rader just in time. He claimed he was preparing to murder his eleventh victim, a woman just three houses down from his own home. He said it would be his grand finale, where he would hang the woman upside down, then set her house on fire for a sensational, dramatic effect. Dennis Rader was going to go out as the most famous killer of all time. All he needed was a fireworks show and some circus jugglers.

Tim Relph did not just stalk and help arrest Rader. He also testified against him in court, then interviewed him in jail. Today, besides chasing his second serial killer, Relph teaches law enforcement classes at Wichita State University, where the subject his students want to discuss often turns to serial killers, and the BTK and I-70 cases in particular. Relph warns them that these cases are not solved overnight. "I tell them, if you are going to get into this business, you are going to have unsolved cases. You have to keep your radar up and keep looking. You have got to keep your head in the game."

I wanted to know if Relph learned anything from Dennis Rader that might help him in his pursuit of the I-70 killer. Could anything be gleaned from interviewing someone like Rader that might help any homicide detective going forward? "These two men are very different killers," Relph says. "You are not going to find somebody who thinks like a Dennis Rader, or thinks like a Ted Bundy. One gives you hope for the other, for sure. But comparing Dennis Rader to the I-70 killer, their motivations are so completely different. Rader killed over many years. This guy is killing in such a compact time."

Besides their motivations and time frames, there is something else completely different about the BTK killer and the I-70 killer: the need for attention. The BTK killer was starved for it. The I-70 killer is a phantom.

Relph believes if there is any similarity between Dennis Rader and the I-70 killer, it has to do with some sort of traumatic event in their lives. Something that made them pop. "Where Rader pauses from killing," Relph says, "you can see events in his life that dictated that. With the I-70 killer, that has always certainly been the thought, that there was some kind of life distress or some kind of traumatic psychological event that caused him to unleash that fury in such a short period of time."

So Relph, like other homicide detectives in Indianapolis, Terre Haute, Raytown, and St. Charles, keeps digging, waiting for that day when the right tip, or something like a floppy disk, might fall in their lap. "At the time when that tip comes in, it is all hands on deck. You can get all kinds of excited. But knowing who did it, that is just a part of it. If you want to push something through prosecution, that is just the start."

I told Relph that his job would be much easier if all serial killers thought the same way.

"None of them really think the same way," Relph said. Then he laughed. "Thank God."

I thanked Relph for his time, and told him to get some sleep. As he turned to walk away, I looked back at him. I expected him to turn around and say, "Oh, Bob, there is just one more thing..."

But I knew Relph was not heading to bed. Columbo had a double homicide to solve.

CHAPTER 8
"Are there serial killers everywhere in Indiana…"

Like Tim Relph in Wichita, Brad Rumsey grew up in Crown Point, Indiana haunted by his own serial killer. The cozy northern Indiana town known for its annual corn roast festival was about to get an unwanted visitor.

Larry Eyler is believed to have murdered more than 20 young men, most of them connected to the gay community, between 1982 and 1984. Eyler was known as "The Interstate Killer," as the bodies of his victims were spread across highways throughout the Midwest.

Eyler stalked the Midwest searching for victims. One of Eyler's first victims was a man named Craig Townsend, who was found drugged, beaten, naked, and comatose in a rural field in Crown Point.

Rumsey eventually headed 150 miles south to study at Indiana State University in Terre Haute.

Larry Eyler would also settle down in Terre Haute. Soon, a man named Steven Agan disappeared from Terre Haute. His body was found mutilated.

Eyler would later be stopped for a routine traffic violation. With him was a young hitchhiker. Police searched his truck and found a buffet of weapons: a knife with blood on it, nylon rope, a hammer, handcuffs, surgical tape, a mallet, and baseball bats. His boot impressions matched those at one of the murder scenes. Police would later search his residence, where they found a key that was a duplicate of a key on Steven Agan's body. Eyler was charged with murder, but proclaimed his innocence.

And then the police case crumbled. The search of Eyler's home was done without a search warrant. Larry Eyler was set free. Detectives in the case were furious. One described Eyler as "charming and polite" until nightfall, when "he is the macho, beer drinking, homosexual type."

Eyler then moved from Terre Haute to Chicago, where he soon killed again, dismembering the body of 16-year-old Daniel Bridges, who had been cut into eight pieces with a saw. His remains were found in a garbage dump near where Eyler was living. Inside Eyler's blood-stained apartment, police found Daniel Bridges' clothes, saturated with blood. Eyler's fingerprints were found on the various body bags, and multiple eyewitnesses said they saw him put the bags in the dumpster. Police discovered that Eyler would keep the shirts of his victims as souvenirs.

Larry Eyler again claimed his innocence. The state went for the death penalty, and it only took the jury three hours to find Eyler guilty. He was sentenced to die by lethal injection.

In prison, Eyler then penned a letter to Illinois Governor Jim Thompson, offering to share the names of his victims in exchange for a life sentence. And Eyler had another offer: he would name an accomplice who committed the murders with him. "I can never undo what I have done," Eyler wrote. "But I do believe that I have good qualities."

In a desire to close the cases, get a confession, and look for an accomplice, officials accepted Eyler's offer. Eyler would eventually confess to more than 20 murders, even bragging about his accomplishment. That of course surprised his mother, Shirley deKoff, who described her son as "a friendly, helpful boy who was incapable of hurting anyone."

But Larry Eyler's story did not end here. He said the accomplice was a man named Robert Little. The pair of gay men had lived together for 9 years. Eyler said Little was like Charles Manson, and he pushed Eyler to find victims for the pair. Eyler claimed the two of them would bring young men ome for bondage and murder, with Little doing the killing, while Eyler took pictures. Larry Eyler passed a polygraph test when he was questioned about Little. The State moved quickly, and charged Little with first degree murder in the death of Agan.

To shock the world even more, Robert Little was a respected professor at Indiana State University, heading up the Library Science Department. The town of Terre Haute and the campus at Indiana State was rocked.

When the trial began, Eyler took the witness stand and spilled the beans on Little. When the state asked Eyler to describe the Stephen Agan murder, Eyler said Little complained that the murder took place "too fast." In his closing argument, defense attorney Dennis Zahn stared at the jury, then pointed at Larry Eyler, and asked one question: "Would you convict an honorable man on the word of Larry Eyler?" The jury would not. Little was found not guilty, and went back to teaching at Indiana State.

Before Eyler faced the needle, he died in prison from AIDS complications. But still today, Eyler victims are turning up. 19-year-old William Lewis went missing 40 years ago. Remains that were found were recently identified as him, with DNA on the scene matching Eyler.

Brad Rumsey was watching this unfold long before he put on a badge. "First, it was Larry Eyler," Rumsey said. "Then we had Herb Baumeister in Indianapolis. And then the I-70 serial killer arrives in our backyard. It was like 'are there serial killers everywhere in Indiana?'"

According to the FBI, there are up to 50 serial killers roaming the streets of America at any given time. They kill up to 150 people in a typical year. Thus, the average serial killer is killing three people per year. Fortunately for

Brad Rumsey, it only appears that all of them are in his neighborhood. "Being born and raised in Indiana, it hits close to home." Rumsey said. "And it was not just Crown Point and Indiana State for me. My brother also went to Indiana State, and he was there right at the time of the I-70 serial killer." Rumsey paused and chuckled. "It is like I can't get away from them."

CHAPTER 9
"If you can work on a case like this and not get personally involved, what the hell is wrong with you?"

If you google "grizzled homicide detective," surely a picture of Patrick McCarrick will pop up. For 41 years, he proudly wore the badge of the St. Charles Police Department. When it came time for McCarrick to retire, he looked at the calendar. He remembered the exact date he was hired: December 15, 1973. He looked again at his suggested retirement date: November 2014. "That is just not going to work, fellas," McCarrick told his bosses. "I need to work a few more weeks. I am not leaving here until I finish the job I started." He finished the job on December 14. Exactly 41 years to the date.

Finishing the job has always mattered to McCarrick, who has overseen numerous homicide investigations in his career, including the cases of Nancy Kitzmiller and the I-70 serial killer. He has commandeered Major Case Squad investigations in the St. Louis area, leading a team of special homicide investigators on the most difficult to solve cases. You spend some time with McCarrick, and you soon realize you are dealing with a man defined by his passion, even years after his retirement.

A task force, including FBI and DNA experts, was going to look at the I-70 serial killer again. "I was not going to miss that," McCarrick said.

He walks slowly with a cane now, but he carries a mind as sharp as a steel trap. "The Kitzmiller case is the essence of why we exist as a police department," McCarrick said, pounding his fist on the table. "You do not forget a case like this. Ever. You do not give up on a case like this. Ever. If we do not do this case right, the other things we do on a daily basis really do not matter very much. A case like this is the reason we exist as a police department."

The Kitzmiller case landed in McCarrick's lap in 1993, one year after Nancy's murder at the Boot Village store. By that time, police knew about Indianapolis, Wichita, and Terre Haute. They were not telling the public, but they knew that they were dealing with both a serial killer and a madman. "We had a few suspects in and out of the investigation over many years. Within a short amount of time we knew that all of the ballistics at all of the scenes matched, so we knew it was the same guy. We concluded from that evidence that this guy's motive was solely the act of the killing, and nothing else."

The first part of the investigation was determining who might have been in the immediate area at the time of the murders. "We did a lot of work in the early part of the Kitzmiller investigation looking into people who had an opportunity to commit the crime," McCarrick said. "We did a lot of work locating people who may have been in the area at the time. We had thousands and thousands of names of people we could put at or near the scene of the crime." This would include hotel records, food and gas receipts, and anybody who used a credit card within hours of St. Charles. McCarrick then laughed. "To show you how thorough we were, we even had Kevin Costner's name. We are pretty confident he did not do it."

"Kevin Costner?" I laughed. "I can see it now. He asked you if this was heaven, and you said no, it was St. Charles!"

McCarrick laughed. He said there were a couple of leads early on. "We had probably a dozen what you might call 'persons of interest,' but none of them really panned out."

McCarrick soon discovered that some of those possible suspects became a little too interested in the case. "We had several people call us and claim they were responsible for the crime. They could not wait to confess. They all wanted to be known as the I-70 serial killer. I remember we went to the Leavenworth, Kansas prison one day to interview this guy who claimed to be the killer. We knew he was in the St. Charles area at the time of the murder, and we think he may have committed a robbery in the same shopping plaza that Nancy worked in just a few weeks earlier. But we could tell the guy was just using us. He wanted to be executed, it made him a big man in prison, and he needed to be convicted of some murder in order to be put on death row. I was pretty confident he did not do it." Years later, determined to die, that same prisoner hung himself in an Indiana jail cell.

For a detective that has seen just about everything over the years, the I-70 killer has thrown some curveballs into McCarrick's murder investigation textbook. "These were extremely high risk crimes that this killer did," McCarrick said. "Very unusual to say the least. If you are going to do a robbery in a high risk situation, and you are after the money, you are going to rob a bank or a grocery store. You go into a shoe store at two o'clock on a Sunday afternoon, how much are you expecting to get? You are not going to get very much money. We concluded from that that this guy's killing motive was not robbery. He was not after the money. His only motive was simply the act of the killing."

Like other detectives, McCarrick is stumped by the serial killer's mode of transportation. He just vanishes into thin air, like a phantom, with no getaway vehicle in sight. "He had to have a vehicle somewhere. He could not just walk around for long. He had to have some sort of transportation nearby to get out of there. How he always managed to get away without being seen is a real mystery, not just in St. Charles, but everywhere."

McCarrick paused when asked if he could ever recall such a similar, heinous crime. "This one is certainly very unique. I think there are some parallels between this case and the Unabomber case, because that went on for so long and in so many different places and with so many different victims."

For 17 years, from 1978 to 1995, Ted Kaczynski, the "Unabomber," killed three people and injured 23 others after sending bombs in the mail targeting people he thought were advancing modern technology. Kaczynski was eventually turned in by his own family, and police found him living in the Montana wilderness.

∽

This is not McCarrick's first dance with a serial killer. He was on the hunt back in 1980 when Anthony LaRette was raping and murdering dozens of women across the country during a span that lasted three decades. LaRette's last victim was eighteen-year-old Mary Fleming of St. Charles. Waiting for LaRette was Pat McCarrick.

It was a little before noon on the morning of July 25, 1980. Fleming, soaked in blood, ran across the street from her house and collapsed on a neighbors doorstep. She was naked except for a bikini top. Her neck had been slashed from ear to ear, and she had been stabbed several times in the chest. Fleming's body showed signs of a fierce struggle with her assailant, as she had multiple bruises and cuts. Emergency crews rushed to the scene, but could not save Fleming before she bled to death. St. Charles police would find blood scattered throughout her apartment. A witness said they saw a man run from the apartment, get into a cream-colored convertible, and quickly drive away. St. Charles police traced the car to a man named Richard Roberson, who told them it was his car, but he had let LaRette borrow the car from him earlier that day for a job interview. Two days after the murder, LaRette fled St. Charles for his home in Kansas.

Detectives arranged for Roberson to call LaRette, while they listened on another line. During that phone call, LaRette admitted to Roberson that he killed Fleming. He would later confess to police, saying he was burglarizing Fleming's apartment when she unexpectedly walked in on him.

McCarrick's dogged pursuit of LaRette would not go unnoticed. He appeared on the television show *On the Case with Paula Zahn.*

Anthony LaRette would be executed in 1995. Before being put to death, he admitted to killing more than a dozen victims in eleven states. "The last crime he committed was right here in St. Charles," McCarrick said. "And we caught him. The best thing that we can do in a murder case is stop the guy so that he can't hurt anybody else."

As years went by, McCarrick went looking outside the box for the I-70 killer. When detectives matched ballistics used in the I-70 killings to a rare old German Navy pistol, McCarrick went looking for one, and bought it. When Reddit readers began discussing the I-70 case, McCarrick reached out to them, determined to gather any information they could add to the investigation. And when retirement time came calling for McCarrick, he asked to remain in the loop with other detectives working on the I-70 case.

Today, with decades passed without an answer, McCarrick insists he is still hopeful. "I would not characterize this case as cold, because we have never stopped working on it for almost 30 years. And I think we are going to get this. I really do. All we need is a name, and we can get this guy."

The Boot Village store would close soon after Nancy Kitzmiller was killed. It would re-open to other tenants as the years went by. Today, the Panera Bread is bustling with hundreds of customers walking through the door each day. One of them was McCarrick, who was going there to pick up dinner one night when he stopped in his tracks and stared at the store. It all came back to him.

"What did that feel like?" I asked him.

"Like turning back the clock," he said.

"I decided the heck with my dinner. I just walked in and asked one of the girls who was working there if I could talk to the manager. I think she thought I wanted to complain about something. The manager came out and said, 'How can I help you?' I told him, 'I am a retired policeman. I worked on a case that happened here many years ago, where someone was killed. I would like to go in the back room for a minute where the killing happened if that is okay.' He said, 'Oh, you mean that girl.' He was probably only around ten years old at the time Nancy was murdered, but he remembered the case. He said, 'Sure come on, I will take you back there.' And I walked back there in the back room where Nancy was killed. I looked around back there and thought about DNA, and how much technology has changed and how it might keep changing in the future. Something in that room might still solve the case someday."

Some detectives, after fifty years on the streets, might balk at change and technology. Not Patrick McCarrick. "Things are a lot different now than they were 30 years ago. We can do things now that we never even dreamed of 30 years ago. We really think the science is going to solve this case and catch this guy. It is more than just DNA. It is science and technology. All we need is that name. If we get the name, we can put the case on this guy." McCarrick paused. The passion came back to his face. "Every case is as bad as it can get. We can fix a lot of things but we can't fix dead."

It has been nearly nine years now since McCarrick laid down his police badge for the final time, but there is zero chance he will ever be forgotten in the halls of the St. Charles Police Department. "Captain McCarrick worked tirelessly on this investigation and followed up thousands of potential leads," said St. Charles Police Chief

Ray Juengst. "Although retired, we at the department are fortunate to be able to call on the Captain for insight and suggestions as we move forward on the I-70 serial killer investigation."

And make no mistake about it, if this case is ever solved, the grizzled homicide detective will have played a part. "Because of his diligence and hard work," Juengst said, "he has provided a solid foundation for this case, which our current investigators continue to build on. This would not have been a possibility without the work of the Captain and other investigators invested in this case over the past 30 years. And Pat continues his dedication to our department."

And for the detective that refused to walk away from the job a month early years ago, there is still no walking away now. The Nancy Kitzmiller case, and the hunt for the I-70 killer, is personal to Patrick McCarrick. "You hear people say you should not get personally involved in a case. Well, if you can work on a case like this and not get personally involved, what the hell is wrong with you? I do not want you working for me."

We got up to say goodbye. McCarrick reached for his cane, and we walked slowly to our cars. But his mind? Patrick McCarrick's mind is still faster than any serial killer's could ever be.

CHAPTER 10
"I just remember thinking 'that is kind of odd that you would do that in a family restaurant...'"

Like the other victims of the I-70 serial killer, Sarah Blessing had so much to live for. An honors student in both high school and college, she began her own business in the family living room. She had just finished writing a children's book, and had several poems published, and seemed to have an interest in just about everything, from dancing to basketball.

As our crew prepared to leave Raytown, we noticed some people had gathered in the shopping center to watch us interview Tim Hickman and Chris Shrout. And then a woman approached us. "These are for you," she said. "Thank you for coming." And she handed us a box of doughnuts.

"Thank you," I said, handing the box to Chuck, who I knew would take good care of them.

"You are here for that poor girl who was killed," she said.

"We are," I told her. "How did you know?"

"It is all over Facebook this morning," she answered. "Somebody saw your crew here, and we figured it must have been about that serial killer."

"Yes ma'am," I told her.

"Well, I just wanted to thank you for keeping her memory alive," she said.

"Did you know her?" I asked.

"Oh no," the woman said. "That was a very long time ago. So sad."

I thanked her again and we started up the car to leave. Then a car pulled up next to us, and a man rolled down his window. "Are you the folks doing a story on the serial killer?" he asked.

"Yes sir, I am," I said. "How did you know?" The man looked nervous, and I wondered what he wanted.

"I saw on Facebook that you were coming out here today," he said.

I nodded. There was a pause. "I was here that day," he finally said. I just looked at him. Police had told me they were not aware of any additional witnesses in Raytown.

"Did you talk to the police?" I asked.

"No, I never did," he said.

I gave the man the Raytown Police Department telephone number.

"Did you know Sarah?" I asked.

"No, I did not," he said.

"Will you talk to me?" I asked. "Can you tell me what you saw?"

He said no, but thanked me for coming and doing the story. He prepared to leave, then suddenly turned off his car and stepped out. "Do you have to use my name?" he asked.

"No," I said.

After a long pause, he said, "Okay, I will tell you what I saw. Let's walk over there."

The man pointed to Ginger's restaurant, just a few doors down from Blessing's store, at the other end. We began walking. "I was eating my dinner at Ginger's restaurant," the man said. "It was still early in the evening, and it was just starting to get busy there that night. I remember watching this guy walking in and he is just looking around, like he was scanning the restaurant. I saw a waitress walk up to him and told him he could just sit anywhere he wanted to, and someone would come by to wait on him. The man did not even acknowledge her. He just looked at her and then he turned around and just walked out. I just remember thinking, 'that is kind of odd that you would do that in a family restaurant.' There were plenty of tables available for him to pick from, but like I said, he just turned, left, and walked out the door. It was like he was scanning the joint. He was maybe around six feet tall, and very well dressed. It was very chilling when

I think back about it. I remember just having a very odd feeling about the guy anyway. When I heard about the murder, I just always in my mind wondered if that was him. You think to yourself, 'was that the guy?' It is kind of chilling to think you might have been that close to the guy. It is a mystery I hope someday gets solved."

I tried to ask the man a few more questions. "I can't," he said. "That is all I can say. All I really know is what I saw in this restaurant. But I am pretty sure I saw the killer. It still bothers me." I looked at the man and thought again of Tim Hickman, two men haunted by a few seconds in time 30 years ago.

I thanked the man. We shook hands and I reminded him to call the police and tell them his story. Then my crew and I pulled out of Raytown.

CHAPTER 11
"I would be feeling a little uncomfortable right now if I was him…"

As the winter chill struck and the calendar neared 2022, anyone and everyone who was involved in the hunt for the I-70 serial killer gathered at the Ameristar Casino in St. Charles and swapped notes, files, and stories. Handshakes were everywhere, some from friends who had worked the case for decades, others from new detectives who were welcomed with open arms. Some, like Chris Shrout from Raytown and Raymond Floyd from St. Charles, were among those new to the case. Pat McCarrick of St. Charles was older and long retired. While others like Brad Rumsey of Terre Haute and Don Stepp of St. Charles, had retirement knocking on their front door. Some, like Tim Relph from Wichita, came alone. Others, like Roger Spurgeon from Indianapolis, brought teams.

There was so much work to be done. Shrout and McCarrick, separated by some 40 years, pulled up chairs in the front row, tuned into every word. For Shrout, it was time to learn from all those who went before him; for McCarrick, it was about the case that he has never forgotten, and to pass along whatever information he could to those behind him.

For Roger Spurgeon, it was about Robin Fuldauer and her sister Susan. For Tim Relph, it was about the two Patricias, Magers and Smith, and Magers' husband Mark. For Brad Rumsey, it was about Michael McCown, and his sisters Cynthia and Teresa. For Chris Shrout, it was about Sarah Blessing, as well as for Tim Hickman who remains haunted to this day. And for McCarrick and Stepp, it was about Nancy Kitzmiller, and her parents Don and Carol. 1992 may have been a long time ago, but to the people in this room, especially those who lived and breathed the case for the past 30 years, it has never been far from their minds.

Cold? Yes it is cold. Frozen? It will never be frozen.

And to all of the men and women corralled into that conference room in St. Charles, this was the chance to take one last stab at a case that has befuddled investigators across the country since the day the killer first struck in Indianapolis. And they all recognized that it very likely may be their last, and best chance.

And this gathering all started with a police officer who had watched the case for decades from afar. It was certainly no surprise that Raymond Floyd has spent his entire adult life carrying a gun and wearing a badge. His father, Jack, spent his life in law enforcement and served as the Police Chief in Bowling Green, Missouri for 30 years. His mother, Joanne, was a police dispatcher for 25 years. His wife, Kim, has 25 years in law enforcement.

ᥱᦾ

Raymond Floyd is one hundred and one percent police officer. He began his career as an entry level patrol officer in tiny Louisiana, Missouri. From there he moved on to the Troy, Missouri Police Department where he served for nearly 30 years, and expected to retire. But when an opening occurred in St. Charles, a larger community just down the road, Floyd was intrigued. And he remembered Nancy Kitzmiller and the I-70 serial killer. "I guess you could say I wanted a challenge," Floyd said. "Well, I got myself one."

He applied and then accepted the job in St. Charles in 2020. Just months into his new gig, his thoughts kept coming back to Kitzmiller, the I-70 serial killer, and the story he had followed for years from a distance. Floyd decided to knock on the door of Police Chief Ray Juengst with a request: Was there any chance Floyd could take one last look at the I-70 killer case?

Juengst asked him what he had in mind. Floyd told him he wanted to form a task force, bring everyone together one last time, and incorporate new DNA testing into the investigation. Juengst knew the case was old and cold. But he also knew how much it mattered to the St. Charles community, its police officers, and the Nancy Kitzmiller family. Juengst never balked. "Go for it," he told Floyd.

Raymond Floyd is not the type of man who takes a long time to get the ball rolling. "I knew when I got here that this case had not been looked at for quite a long time," said Floyd. "The last time was in 2004 when they sent in their last lab submissions."

∾

And now, less than one year into his service at St. Charles, and nearly 20 years since the I-70 case had a meeting of the minds, Raymond Floyd was leading a three-state, five-city task force chasing down a serial killer from 30 years ago. And he is determined. "But just because we did not have a task force before did not mean we were not following up on leads."

Floyd quickly picked up the phone and started dialing. Spurgeon in Indianapolis. Relph in Wichita. Rumsey in Terre Haute. Shrout in Raytown. Could we all get together one more time, and give this one last shot? Floyd asked. And how soon? "You bet we can, and how about now?" was the reply he heard across the country.

❦

Floyd smiled. "I got a buy-in from all of the agencies involved in the case. Nobody balked. Everybody wants this case solved, and this killer brought to justice." And thus, the I-70 task force was born, meeting over two days in St. Charles. "It was our concern that if we did not act now, this case could fall to the wayside," Floyd said. "It was now or never is how we looked at it."

❦

When everyone arrived, Floyd led the charge. A new portal was built for all the departments to work together. Information would now be shared instantly with everyone involved. A tip called into Wichita would be seen in Terre Haute. Items stored deep in basements from each murder site would be sent to DNA labs for new testing. They were a team now. The heat was being turned up on a serial killer case that had long gone ice cold.

❦

For most people in the conference room, veterans and rookies, excitement revolved around DNA technology, or specifically, advanced DNA methods that were not available 30 years ago. They were told DNA held the key now, and whatever items they had tucked away in those basements from 30 years ago needed to now be put in play. Detectives began looking over their crime scene notes, and calling back home to see what evidence they still had in their storage rooms. Phone numbers from various testing labs around the country were being passed around the room. Money would need to be found from somewhere to pay for this.

When DNA expert Jami Harmon of Sorenson Forensics rose to speak, you could hear a pin drop. "Go back to when this case first occurred," Harmon told her attentive audience. "In 1992, DNA labs were just switching from the older, longer method of DNA testing to this newer, faster method. It would become a game changer for future crime cases."

That game changer was called "handler," or touch DNA. Not an option in 1992. And Harmon was ready to teach the class.

Tim Relph could not contain his smile. He knew that he still had the wedding veil that the killer in Wichita used to wrap around his gun, hoping to make less noise. A wedding veil that might make all the difference in the world 30 years later.

Brad Rumsey smiled too. He had Mick McCown's pants, where the wallet was missing. Perhaps the killer had rummaged through them.

It was a new ballgame now.

❧

"Look at all these cold cases that are twenty, thirty, forty years old that are now being solved by new advancements in DNA technology," Floyd said. "We are now optimistic that we can pull a DNA profile from one of the five crime scenes. And then we can make a case."

Thirty years seems like a long time. But consider the Boston Strangler, who murdered thirteen women in the 1960s. In 2013, some 51 years after Anna Slessers was the first victim of the Strangler, police exhumed the long deceased body of Albert DeSalvo for DNA testing, and tied him to another Strangler victim, Mary Sullivan. Age meant nothing to that killer. His victims ranged from 19 to 85, killed inside their own apartments, without any sign of a struggle. Some women left town. Others bought tear gas. Boston police were on the lookout for maintenance men or delivery men. Turns out DeSalvo sometimes told the women he was a detective, or a motorist with car problems.

DeSalvo confessed and was sentenced to life in prison, but escaped, even leaving the prison superintendent a goodbye note. He was captured the next day, and was later stabbed to death in prison.

Albert DeSalvo had been in the ground for 40 years. And DNA still caught him.

Meanwhile in St. Charles, there were heads shaking in the room, mostly because nothing with their serial killer made sense. Robbery was not a motive. There were no sexual assaults. There were not even crime scene struggles. There was never a sign of any vehicle. Composite sketches were pretty generic. He was using an antique German target shooting pistol as his weapon. And who drives 1,200 miles back and forth between Indianapolis and Wichita to randomly kill someone?

I approached Tim Relph during a break in the meeting. The trip to Wichita had everyone stumped. Of all the crazy stuff that did not make sense, the Wichita journey was at the top of the list.

"I am not even sure he knew when he was going to kill next," Relph said. "Just makes no sense. No sense at all."

When the news media began reporting about the task force meeting behind closed doors, the tips quickly came pouring in. "We received dozens and dozens of calls after that first task force meeting," said Detective Kelly Rhodes from St. Charles. "Here in St. Charles, we received so many tips. The phone calls came flooding in. And every single phone call that we get we look into."

And it was not just happening in St. Charles. In Indianapolis, where the serial killer struck first, the calls also came pouring in when word of the task force meeting leaked out. "I was really surprised by one," said Homicide Detective Columbus Ricks. "It was a woman who was fairly close to the incident when it occurred and she had no idea what was going on until she heard about the task force. She saw it and she called and said, 'I had no idea what was going on and this is what I saw.'"

❧

"We received 50-60 new leads since our meeting began," Floyd said after the task force meeting ended. "There is no crime that is perfect. Killers make mistakes. This case will never die in St. Charles." And one of those leads has detectives now sitting on the edge of their seats. "We have a lead that we have characterized as a Number 1," Floyd said.

Floyd would not go any further, except to say a Number 1 is the highest priority lead possible. Now, Floyd and the task force cross their fingers and wait for a possible DNA match. And if it comes, detectives across the Midwest are more than ready to roll. "If we get a hit on the DNA, we are not going to throw a high five or a party. That is when the work starts," Relph said.

Like everyone else who has studied this case, Floyd has the same question that may never be answered. "I just can't begin to understand why the killings started in the first place, and why they suddenly stopped so quickly." Of course, they may not have stopped. The I-70 killer may have become the I-35 killer a year later in Texas.

"Texas is a mixed review to me depending on what investigator you talk to," Floyd said. "We have been in contact with the authorities in Texas. They are working on their end to see if they can tie things together, and see if these cases are possibly related. We can't rule it out."

%

In the meantime, Floyd and the task force are not sitting around waiting. They still have plenty of other things to do, as crime never takes a day off. "Like I said..." Floyd laughed. "Not a day goes by that I am not working on this case in some form. No matter what else is going on, I am going to be right here digging." And his digging never stopped. He teamed up with a database company and began searching. Everything they could find in Indianapolis, Wichita, Terre Haute, St. Charles, and Raytown.

And Floyd thought they might have found a goldmine. "I was told 'if you can ever find somebody who was in all these towns on the days of the murders, you've got your killer.'"

Floyd found a man who was in Wichita the day before Patricia Smith and Patricia Magers were killed, and then in St. Charles the day before Nancy Kitzmiller was murdered. While there was no connection to the other three cities, it was enough for Floyd to keep digging. He found the man living in Chicago, got in his car, and headed north. But the man had relatives in both towns, and was there for family events.

"I am [now] convinced it was not him," Floyd said. "But when we first saw the connection..."

If the I-70 killer is out there somewhere, and he is laughing at what he has gotten away with so far, Floyd said he has a little friendly advice for the man. "I would be feeling a little uncomfortable right now if I was him."

CHAPTER 12
"Not a very usual weapon of choice…"

In Indianapolis, all the detectives could do was scratch their heads and look at each other in amazement over the next shoe that dropped.

In a cold case where absolutely nothing made much sense about the killer or his motives, it may have been the oddest question of all for homicide detectives at the five locations spread across the country to ponder. It almost made the other strange questions seem easy to answer. And of course, they were not.

They already had their hands full.

Why did he kill in the first place? That soon became obvious to everyone working the various homicide scenes. With little or no money taken, and with no known relationships to any of the six victims and no evidence at any scene of any type of sexual abuse, the only real motive police could deduct was the thrill of the kill. There was literally no second option. And no motive made the task for investigators that much more difficult.

How did he get away without any type of transportation in sight? The only plausible explanation is that the killer had a vehicle parked somewhere nearby that he could calmly walk to afterwards, blending into the environment, but definitely not near the scene of the crimes where someone could see him leaving the scene.

Was he not concerned that someone might simply walk in and catch him in his murderous act? See the first question and multiply the thrill. And understand this killer never entered a store if there was a customer anywhere in sight. He obviously staked out his locations and targeted victims in advance, as multiple witnesses in Raytown have stated. Only in Wichita did a customer walk in on the killer, and that was after closing hours.

And then came the gun. A clue to the puzzle so preposterous it would have been laughable if there were not dead bodies across the country. The detectives in Indianapolis were not alone in scratching their heads. None of the detectives spread across the country has an answer about the gun. Not veteran detectives who have worked the case for decades, or any of the sets of new eyes that have inherited the case. "It makes no sense," said Roger Spurgeon of the Indianapolis Police Department.. "Absolutely no sense."

Killers have long chosen ease of use and reliability in selecting the weapon of their choice for their dastardly acts. Why would they not? Homicide scenes often wind up tracing suspects back to semiautomatic pistols, maybe a Ruger 9mm or a Raven Arms 25, perhaps a Lorcin 38, or the most common: a simple Smith and Wesson 38 revolver. But not the I-70 serial killer. His choice for a weapon was off the charts, one so rare that all homicide detectives could do was look at each other and wonder.

Once investigators had their ballistics matches, they considered two possibilities. First, they looked at the Intratec Tec22, also called the Scorpion or Sport 22. But they eventually settled on the Erma Werke ET22, one of the rarest guns a killer could possibly come across. Ammunition for the gun was CCI brand, with copper-clad lead bullets. It seemed impossible to believe at first, but the ballistics trail from Indianapolis to Wichita to Terre Haute to St. Charles to Raytown did not lie. If you have never heard of the Erma Werke ET22, you are certainly not alone. It was originally used by the German Navy in World War I, but they were so unreliable the Germans mainly used them only as target pistols.

"This was certainly an extremely unusual gun," said Detective Tim Relph of the Wichita Police Department. "To say the least."

And the oddity of the Erma Werke did not stop with it being ancient or foreign. It was also prone to jamming and malfunctioning. Oh, and you could not hide it if you tried. "Not a very usual weapon of choice," said Detective Kelly Rhodes of the St. Charles Police Department, "because it is not very easily concealable." That is because the ET22 has a barrel that is almost a foot long. Just about the last gun in the world a killer wants to be seen hauling around.

And the bizarre reasons for the Erma Werke go on and on.

Only about six thousand of the ET22 models were ever made, again starting more than 100 years ago. The final production lines of the gun were run in the 1960s, and from there it is likely where the serial killer's gun came from. The gun had problems on both the feeding and ejecting ends, which eventually led to the jamming and malfunctions issues. They were also notorious for suffering more misfires than fires. Gun collectors say the Erma Werke "was practically made to jam." They add that the Erma Werke is very scarce and is rarely seen even by firearms collectors. And yet somehow it was the weapon of choice for a madman roaming the country with killing on his mind.

An old advertisement from the gun magazine *LA Distributors* had this to say about the Navy Model Erma: "Enjoy inexpensive shooting at its very best with this famous look alike gun, a fast shoot and dependable 22 caliber pistol ideal for plinking, target shooting and pest control."

A look alike gun used for pest control was incredibly the gun of choice for the madman killer and the main piece of evidence for investigators, who were left shaking their heads and wondering not only why and how such a gun landed in the hands of a killer, but how he managed to make it work.

You can buy an Erma Werke today on the internet, but it is so old and rare it might cost you up to a thousand dollars. Was a serial killer shopping for his murder weapon on the internet thirty years ago? Not very likely. eBay was not even around in 1992. Equally not as likely was that he bought one at a gun show, or through a magazine ad, leaving behind a paper trail that police could someday eventually trace. It is possible he could have come across one on the street, but how many street sellers carry an old German Navy pistol among their arsenal? Perhaps our serial killer resorted to a lesser crime, and just stole the gun from somewhere, not even knowing what he was dealing with. But detectives think it was more likely that the gun was passed down to him through the generations by relatives, and held some sort of emotional value to the killer. If that was the case, the gun would have been a prized possession to him, a partner so to speak, in his crime journey. But once he had the gun, however he got it, getting the Erma Werke to work, with all of its problems, would not have been easy.

And then came yet another head scratcher for detectives. Police discovered that each casing at all of the crime scenes was linked to the others by a red substance forensically lifted from the casings, but detectives had no idea what it could possibly be. They sent the casings to the FBI crime lab in Quantico for testing. And while a final analysis could not definitely be determined, FBI investigators speculated that the substance appeared to be some sort of jeweler's red rouge. The killer was apparently rubbing the bullet casings with the rouge and using the corundum to polish the cartridges. This would allow the bullets to slide more easily into the chamber. For detectives, feeling the need to polish the bullets is a clear sign that the I-70 killer was assembling his own homemade guns. It also led detectives to speculate that the killer quite possibly worked in an environment in which the rouge was used. Now they were checking jewelry stores in Indianapolis, Wichita, Terre Haute, St. Charles, and Raytown.

"He was probably some sort of a collector of weapons," Tim Relph surmised. "He probably had several of them back at home."

Realizing the rare gun held their biggest and so far only real clue, the St. Charles Police Department went on the hunt. They bought the exact Model ET22 used in the murders through an online auction. It still sits in an evidence box at the police department. They then communicated with gun enthusiasts around the world on web pages, asking anyone with information about the gun to please come forward. Even today, they are placing ads in gun magazines, reaching out to new readers who might not be aware of what happened 30 years ago. They have left no stone unturned in their pursuit of information about the Erma Werke Model ET22.

And then suddenly police had a possible lead on the gun. A construction worker in Indianapolis said a cream-colored Cadillac Eldorado with Florida plates quickly sped up to his work zone, and a man jumped out and excitedly ran up to him asking about work. The worker told the man to follow him down the street to the company office to fill out an application.

As they arrived at the office, the worker saw a woman in the passenger seat of the Cadillac hand the man a rifle. The worker thought he might be in danger, so he quickly got back in his car and fled. The couple in the Cadillac began following him. The worker became more frightened, and headed into a wooded area, parked, and hid. He never saw the Cadillac again, but called the police. He saw police cars with their lights on drive by where he was, but they never stopped.

Because it was 3pm, and they were heading to the Payless Shoe Store.

Indianapolis police brought the man in for an interview. "Did you see the rifle clearly?" they asked. "Could you pick it out if we showed you a lineup of rifles?"

The detectives knew the chances of the man picking out the rare Erma Werke Model ET22, the German navy target pistol from World War 1, were basically zero. They showed him a lineup with numerous rifles.

He immediately picked out the Erma Werke.

"He was very believable," said a detective working the case. "It was a viable lead then, and still is now."

Detectives began checking all registrations for Florida Cadillac Eldorados. But nothing turned up.

And then, police made a devastating mistake in their investigation, one that haunts them to this day. After much internal debate, the St. Charles Police Department made the decision to go public and release information about the Erma Werke to the news media, providing them with a detailed sketch of the gun. This was gobbled up by newspapers and television stations throughout the Midwest. They were appealing to anyone who might know anything about the rare gun to come forward, hoping that their aggressive approach would bring in new leads. At first glance, it made sense. But in retrospect, that decision to go public proved to be a crucial mistake early in the investigation.

Pat Morici, the commander of the Major Case Squad on the Nancy Kitzmiller case, remembers how livid he was when he first heard about the gun information being released to the public. "Seriously? Are you kidding me? You just told a serial killer you knew what his weapon was!" Morici said. "If this guy was going to keep killing, he was obviously going to change guns now. There goes your ballistics matches to other possible cases, and there goes your chance to tie any other cases to the I-70 case. Why would you show the killer your hand? It was just a very bad mistake by the police department."

Captain John O'Rando, working with detectives on the Major Case Squad, also remembers the discord at the time between the St. Charles Police Department and the Major Case leadership. "You had the St. Charles Police Department releasing information on their own, and then you had the Major Case Squad coming in and trying to clean it up. I remember there was quite a heated debate in the room after the gun information was released to the public. To put that information out there about the gun for the killer to see? That was surprising to say the least. We were very surprised. And not very happy."

Terre Haute detective Brad Rumsey agreed. "When you go back and look at the overall big picture, you have to consider how the case was handled by the police back then. Instead of telling the world the cases were connected because of ballistics, they could have simply said the mode of operation was very similar. But instead they told the bad guy 'we know it is the same gun.' So of course now he is going to switch guns if he is going to continue to commit these crimes."

Detective Raymond Floyd with the St. Charles Police Department looks back at that decision and acknowledges a mistake was made. "After the last murder in Raytown that information about the cases being linked was released to the news media. And after that information was released that weapon was never used again in another murder."

It was probably not a coincidence.

On the other hand, one could make the case that releasing the information about the gun scared off the killer, made him stop his murderous spree, and perhaps kept others alive.

St. Charles Detective Pat McCarrick says police work has now moved past the gun. "We are not as focused on information about the gun today as we were thirty years ago. Now this case is all about science and technology. At the end of the day, that is what we believe is going to solve this case."

With very few leads on the gun after all of the publicity, other detectives agree with McCarrick, as police in all five cities have pivoted to science and touch-DNA as their best hope to solve the case.

Eventually, investigators on the I-70 case would reach out to the FBI to conduct a profile on the serial killer. Here is what they had to go on:

a.   the killer appeared to have absolutely no motive, other than the thrill of killing

b.   the killer liked to murder his victims during the busiest times of the day, and in plain sight

c.   the killer seemed to have very little concern if someone walked in during the murders

d.   the killer had no getaway vehicle anywhere in sight of the murder scenes

e.   his weapon of choice was an old German made Navy pistol originally dating to World War I, with a foot long barrel that constantly jammed and malfunctioned

So you always wanted to be an FBI profiler? Because in Quantico, Virginia, that is exactly what they had to deal with.

CHAPTER 13
"This guy likes being named the I-70 serial killer..."

"I grew up a farm boy out in the country in Ohio. I never dreamed in a million years I would have spent my life doing something like this." After all, the job is so rare, the skills so precise, who could predict such a life for anyone?

Larry Ankrom would spend most of that life at the FBI headquarters in Quantico, Virginia, specializing in behavioral science, eventually becoming chief of the FBI's Behavioral Analysis Unit for the western part of the United States. In layman's terms, Ankrom is an FBI profiler. And an extremely expert one. He is widely regarded as one of the top profilers and criminal investigative analysts in the world, having previously been assigned to both the FBI's child abduction and serial killer units.

The first time that an FBI profile was used was back in 1957. It was for the "Mad Bomber" case in New York, where a man named George Metesky was terrorizing the streets of New York City in the 1940s and 1950s. Metesky was setting off explosives throughout the city in libraries, theaters, offices, and bus and subway terminals. The FBI profile came to the conclusion that the suspect would be the following: heavyset, middle aged, foreign, Roman Catholic, single, living with a brother or sister, and he preferred to wear double-breasted suits in public. Incredibly, the profile squarely hit the bullseye except for the fact that Metesky lived with two sisters instead of a brother and sister. When the Mad bomber was arrested, he was wearing a double-breasted suit. It was an amazing piece of work by specialists in a brand new crimefighting field, and opened up a whole new world for crime detectives around the country.

There are common traits that profilers like Ankrom look for when they begin looking at a case. For example, in the I-70 murders, when the killer shoots the victims, it indicates a desire for them to remain remote or distant from the victim. And in the I-70 case, where the killer is in a rush, it is a sign they are likely a younger suspect.

"I have worked on hundreds of serial killer cases," Ankrom said. "There is the profile, and then later, hopefully, there is the interview with the killer after they have been captured and are willing to talk about their crimes. You try to learn something from one case that might help you move on to the next one. But things that seem logical to us are not logical to them."

Among the things that profilers like Ankrom have learned after dealing with serial killers is they are likely 25-35 years old, white males, they kill their victims in the same way, they appear to be charming and likable before killing their victims, they have no arrest histories, they abuse alcohol and drugs, they travel frequently, they follow their crimes in the media, they kill within their own race, and they have likely been interviewed by the police in the serial killings investigation.

The last of those traits is especially interesting. And of course, the key word is "likely." When it comes to serial killers, one size never fits all. Many times, they are spurred by something in their lives, and those things can be polar opposites for one versus the other.

As soon as detectives in Indiana, Missouri, and Kansas realized that they had a serial killer on their hands, they reached out to Quantico, and eventually to Larry Ankrom. "I start by looking for cookie crumbs that the serial killer may have left along the way," Ankrom said. "Early on, I realized that this case in the Midwest was very, very unusual. You just do not see serial killers targeting businesses this way. I think the idea that he could just drive in and pull this off must have really thrilled and excited him. He must have spent a lot of time visualizing and fantasizing about these crimes, picturing them in his mind, over and over and over again."

Investigators found it odd that the killer would pick such busy locations, usually in the middle of the day. But Ankrom thinks it made sense to the killer. "I do not think he even knew what store he was going to head into next. He probably thought more people in the area might help him blend into the scene, and that made him feel more comfortable. And as we have heard from the few witnesses we had, this guy does not look like the bogeyman. There is nothing at all alarming about his mild-mannered appearance."

Ankrom then focused on what he thinks likely happened inside those stores. "He had to know that his first priority was to get in quickly and then get out quickly. His whole MO is in and out. We are talking minutes. He had very limited interactions with any of the victims. But yet he had enough personal skills to convince them that if they just cooperated with him, and went to the back room, that they would be fine. That is why we do not see any signs of a struggle at any of the crime scenes."

And after he kills his victims? "After he kills them I picture him running away quickly," Ankrom says. "His heart is now beating really hard. He probably feels like he has run a marathon. It is very gratifying to him. His thrill then is reliving what happened in his mind, over and over. He then becomes exhausted, and he might need a place to crash and hide out for a few days. He then needs to find out where that place is. This is why the hotel searches in the area[s] of the killings were so important to detectives." But those searches turned up nothing, leading investigators back on the path of a possible truck driver, who could have slept in his rig.

And then came the downtime for the killer. FBI profiles show most killers crave media attention, as opposed to lying low. Remember George Metesky, the New York City mad bomber? He was finally arrested after giving clues about his crime in letters he wrote to a newspaper bragging about himself and his accomplishments. Ditto Dennis Rader in Wichita. No such luck with the I-70 killer, who disappeared from sight.

℘

And, Ankrom says, there is more, which goes to the heart of the killer. "This guy likes being named the I-70 serial killer. Makes him feel like he is really big time. Makes him think he is smarter than the police and everyone else."

But for the killer, there was no downtime to rest after Indianapolis. For some reason, he had to get to Wichita. There is almost no explanation for that, even for Ankrom. "Whatever triggered in his mind," Ankrom said, "he was suddenly and utterly committed, driving hundreds of miles across the country so quickly. It is possible he may have had jobs on the road. I do not think he went to Wichita searching for someone to kill. I think he went there with a purpose."

But to Ankrom, Wichita was clearly different from the other crime scenes because the killer walked into a situation he did not expect, and then a second dose of trouble came when a customer walked in the front door before he could escape. "First, I do not think he expected to find two women when he walked into the Wichita store. Now he has to find a way to tie them up. Second, he smartly tried to keep the noise down by muzzling his gun with a wedding veil. And then third, he is confronted with the customer who walks through the door after the killer thinks the store is closed. This certainly must have shocked him. And what does he tell the late arriving customer? The same thing he probably told every other victim: 'Come with me, all I am going to do is tie you up so I can get out of here.'"

Ankrom paused again. "Everything that happened inside that wedding store was actually pretty darn impressive as it speaks to the killer's abilities. In a very high risk environment with a lot of stress happening, where multiple things did not go as he had planned in his mind, he did not panic. He was surely nervous, but he showed maturity. It is very impressive. This killer is not just some dopey guy. This killer is in control of the situation."

Ankrom thinks the killer was likely very concerned about the witness that got away in Wichita, and may have decided to change his appearance afterwards. And while Ankrom gives the killer credit for the way he handled the Wichita crime scene, he says the killer made some other mistakes going forward. "The high risk nature of these crimes shows us that the killer is really criminally unsophisticated. He showed us consistent patterns, which allowed us to paint a picture and make a profile of him. And as far as his sophistication, a serious killer would never leave shell casings at the crime scene. He left us with some real potential as far as physical evidence at every single scene."

Ah, those cookie crumbs.

"And the wedding veil, where he held the gun in Wichita," Ankrom added. "Someday, that could tell us the story. But we have not yet been very lucky on touch-DNA cases."

Ankrom says the fact that the killer began his spree in Indiana, went to Wichita, then immediately returned to Indiana suggests that he is from the Indiana area.

And then there is the gun. Ankrom is not as convinced as detectives that the killer was using an antique Erma Werke 22 German pistol. "That gun is awfully hard to carry and hide for a man on a murder spree. It has nearly a foot long barrel, and that is not what the witness in Wichita described seeing to detectives there. But if it indeed is the Erma Werke, and I know the police departments believe it is, it is so rare and unusual, that there must be some sort of reason he would choose that gun. He did not pick it up by luck. It must be very important to him. Maybe it is a ceremonial piece for him, or perhaps it was passed down from a family member. That gun would be his emotional partner in his crime spree."

And that gun, Ankrom feels, might ring a bell to the killers' acquaintances. "If that specific gun is so important to him, or has some story behind it, he has probably told somebody about it. Somewhere along the way. Besides that, somebody out there knows this guy's characteristics. We know from the Wichita witness that when the killer got nervous, he kept rubbing his face, over and over, side to side. That is a specific nervous trait. Somebody has seen this man do that before."

And after Raytown, the killings apparently stopped. "There may well have been other cases, elsewhere, that we do not know about or have not been able to tie him to," Ankrom said. "Or it is possible that he was arrested for something else. It is also possible that he is dead. But if he is still alive, and lurking out there, his desire to kill in this fashion, without motive, did not just go away with time. The thrilling feelings he got after murdering these people did not just go away. They never will."

Ankrom estimates that the killer was in his late 20s or early 30s at the time of the I-70 murders, which would put him around 60 today. He believes he either lived or worked in the Indiana area. "Serial killers usually start in their comfort zone, have some sort of a problem somewhere, then return back to their comfort zone. This guy started in Indianapolis, ventured to Wichita, had a problem, and came right back to Terre Haute. It is textbook."

Ankrom is retired now, having given the I-70 investigation his best shot. He says he still follows the case closely, and is still there for investigators when they reach out. Like everyone else involved, he desperately wants to see a conclusion, and to see how accurate his profile was.

And there is something else Larry Ankrom knows about the I-70 killer. "We also know that he is a coward who specializes in shooting defenseless women in the back of the head."

CHAPTER 14
"Lusk can look forever hell never find me but I am rite under his nose all the time…"

Dear Boss

So now they say I am a Yid when will they lern Dear old Boss! You an me know the truth dont we. Lusk can look forever hell never find me but I am rite under his nose all the time. I watch them looking for me an it gives me fits ha ha I love my work an I shant stop until I get buckled and even then watch out for your old pal Jacky.

Catch me if you Can Jack the Ripper

Sorry about the blood still messy from the last one. What a pretty necklace I gave her.

Delivered to Scotland Yard, September 17, 1888

And so the legacy of serial killers began. It was the late 1880s in the Whitechapel area of London where prostitutes were being murdered. Some 100 years later the Green River Killer would emerge, followed by Charles Manson, Ted Bundy, Wayne Williams, the Zodiac Killer, BTK, Son of Sam, John Wayne Gacy, Jeffrey Dahmer, and many others. The list goes on and on. Hollywood would jump into the fray with movies like *Silence of the Lambs*. Hannibal Lecter became a household name.

In the early part of the 1970s, the United States was hit with a rising wave of homicides, leading the FBI to establish their Behavioral Science Unit. There were 10 original members. They began by working on a central database of known serial killers. The team would travel to various prisons across the country, interviewing serial predators to gather information, trying to compile profiles that might help them down the road. In total, they interviewed 36 prisoners, and began disseminating their information on active cases across the country. By the 1980s, the Behavioral Science Unit split into two sections, one training new cadets at Quantico, and the other helping with ongoing investigations and consultations in the field. And through it all, deep in the halls of Quantico, this profiling began to uncover some very surprising results.

First, contrary to popular belief, serial killers are not a bunch of dysfunctional loners. Most of them are not social misfits, nor do they live alone in their mother's basement. Instead, they are typically your neighbor next door. They usually live in their homes with their families, they have jobs, and they appear on the outside to be normal members of their community. They certainly do not appear to be strange or reclusive. And there is usually no reason for them to appear on a police radar of potential suspects in a homicide case.

Gary Ridgeway, the infamous Green River killer, was married three times, and was currently married when he was finally arrested. He had been employed for more than 30 years. He was an active church member, and spent his time reading the Bible before he confessed to killing 48 women in his spare time in the Seattle area over a 20-year period.

Dennis Rader, the BTK killer, served honorably in the Air Force, was married with children, worked for the local government, was a Boy Scout leader, and was president of his church. It did not stop him from terrorizing Wichita for decades.

John Wayne Gacy married his high school sweetheart, ran three Kentucky Fried Chicken restaurants, served on the board of directors of the local Jaycees, and performed as a clown at local hospitals to entertain hospitalized children. He also killed 33 young men and boys.

It is more than likely that the I-70 killer fits the same mold.

Second, as the I-70 killer has proven, not all serial murders are motivated by sex. One serial killer who appears to have the same motivation as the I-70 killer is John Allen

Muhammad, the notorious Washington DC serial sniper. Muhammad was a former Army Staff Sergeant. Along with Lee Boyd Malvo, the pair killed solely for the thrill of killing, terrorizing the Washington DC area for nearly a month in 2002, driving around and killing 10 people.

Again, the profile fits the I-70 killer.

Third, serial killers are indeed able to stop killing and somehow return to a normal life. "Usually, something dramatic changes in their life," says Ankrom. "It can be something dramatic, or then again it can be something as simple as an increase in their family structure or activities."

Dennis Rader was arrested 14 years after his final killing. We know the I-70 serial killer stopped killing in May of 1992. What detectives do not know is whether he started up again elsewhere, or has been silent since. Both possibilities are clearly still in play.

And finally, there is the perception that serial killers keep killing because they are waiting and hoping to eventually be caught. That does not appear to be the case with most serial killers, and certainly not the I-70 killer. Ankrom says the perception that the serial killer wants to get caught is wrong, especially as it appears in the I-70 case. Rather, as Tim Relph found out with Dennis Rader in Wichita, they believe they are so smart, and certainly smarter than police, that they can't get caught. They do not want to lose the game. It is an ego trip for them, and certainly for the I-70 killer.

"This guy is very confident. He is extremely cocky," said one longtime detective who worked closely on the case and did not want his name used. "He thinks he knows more than everybody else. He certainly thinks he knows more than the police do."

Serial killers may begin with inexperience, but FBI profilers say they gain more confidence with each crime they commit, and then the next scene usually becomes much easier for them. That, of course, was not the case with the I-70 killer, who stumbled into problems at his second killing scene in Wichita. But the I-70 killer's crime scene model was a consistent one, and with that his confidence grew.

What is certain is that serial killers spend much of their time planning their next attack. "It is a fantasy world for them," said Ankrom. "They keep going over their plans in their minds hundreds and hundreds of times in advance. Then they keep going over it again after it happens. It's incredibly exciting for them."

Ankrom emphasizes all of the planning that a serial killer must go through in his mind before he attacks. "It is like people planning a dream vacation," he says. "First these serial killers must target their locations. Then they have to target their victims. Then they have to plan how they will approach the victim. And at some point, they are thinking about how they can control the murder scene."

Ankrom says it is a big puzzle piece for the killers, and a very exciting one. The I-70 killer mastered this by convincing his victims that they would be fine if they just walked into the back room.

Tim Relph has to look no further than Dennis Rader for an example of this. "This is all part of the game they play," Relph said. "It is all part of their thrill."

Profilers say the longer that time goes by for the serial killers without being captured, the more confident they become. They begin to feel invincible. And that, says Ankrom, is when they make mistakes, such as the mistake the I-70 killer made by leaving gun casings at the scenes of all of the murders. And as their crime spree continues, and their confidence grows, serial killers begin to take a few shortcuts and take a few more chances, and thus leave behind more clues for law enforcement, such as the wedding veil the serial killer used to hide his gun in Wichita. "Those cookie crumbs again," said Ankrom.

And sometimes, they plan the perfect crime, determined to kill, only to see something happen that they did not plan on. Frustrated, but not wanting to leave without finishing their much planned out fantasy, they kill anyway. This may certainly have been the case in Terre Haute, when the I-70 killer discovered that Mick McCown was not a woman.

ᑲᕋ

At the end of the day, there is no generic template for a serial killer. There are no common motives. Ted Bundy has little to do with Jeffrey Dahmer. They are not defined by sex, age, race, or religion. The profile is valuable for likelihood and probabilities, but as Tim Relph noted after he interviewed Rader, "none of these guys think alike." However, many times, their actions are alike. And they often exhibit some of the same similar types of behavior. For example, many of them had a very troubled childhood or were abused or neglected by adult figures in their early life.

And no matter how many characteristics profilers try to establish as they search for a serial killer, and no matter how many traits they learn after a killer is captured, profiling is just a tool in the process. Some will certainly argue that speculating into the mind of a serial killer, and for example what his relationship was with his mother when he was a child, has never solved a real life crime investigation. Then again there is David Berkowitz, the infamous "Son of Sam," who profilers say his life unraveled when he learned later in life that his mother gave him away at birth, calling it "the primary crisis" of his life. His killing spree began soon after. Within a few years, Berkowitz would kill six and wound seven others in New York City.

Today, while fictional television shows dramatically hunt down killers with the FBI at their side, reality will show just how difficult it really is, and how specialized the profiling part of the job is. While there are currently more than 13,000 FBI agents across the country, there are only about three dozen profilers. And even if you count those who have retired over the years since FBI profile training began, the number of profilers is only around 50. And for future generations of young people looking to become an FBI profiler someday, the task is enormous and the odds are extreme. An advanced degree and ten years of investigative experience is required. And even then, a 560-hour course awaits you.

Which brings us back to the very first profile: Jack the Ripper.

A Scotland Yard surgeon named Thomas Bond handled the Ripper's profile. He is considered the father of modern profiling. After he examined the mutilated bodies of the victims, Dr. Bond deduced that the killer had to be a male, and that he must have had an anatomical understanding, perhaps even surgical skills.

Bond wrote this in his report to police:

> The murderer must have been a man of physical strength and of great coolness and daring. There is no evidence that he had an accomplice. He must in my opinion be a man subject to periodical attacks of Homicidal and erotic mania. The character of the mutilations indicate that the man may be in a condition sexually, that may be called satyriasis. It is of course possible that the Homicidal impulse may have developed from a revengeful or brooding condition of the mind, or

that Religious Mania may have been the original disease, but I do not think either hypothesis is likely. The murderer in external appearance is quite likely to be a quiet inoffensive looking man probably middle aged and neatly and respectably dressed. I think he must be in the habit of wearing a cloak or overcoat or he could hardly have escaped notice in the streets if the blood on his hands or clothes were visible.

Assuming the murderer to be such a person as I have just described he would probably be solitary and eccentric in his habits, also he is most likely to be a man without regular occupation, but with some small income or pension. He is possibly living among respectable persons who have some knowledge of his character and habits and who may have grounds for suspicion that he is not quite right in his mind at times.

As panic spread through the streets of London, there were those who even came to suspect Bond was Jack the Ripper. Thomas Bond would later commit suicide, hurling himself out of his bedroom window.

⌘

There were 11 murders over a three-year period in the Whitechapel area that police were never able to solve. At least five of the victims were tied to the man dubbed Jack The Ripper. And like the I-70 killer, Jack the Ripper worked very quickly, killing all of his victims within a month's time. And then he apparently stopped. Unlike the I-70 killer, Jack the Ripper did not travel very far. All of his victims were murdered within a mile of each other. Whoever the killer was in the 1880s, he made Jack the Ripper go down in history. And he tortured the London police.

> *Dear Boss,*
>
> *I keep on hearing the police have caught me but they wont fix me just yet. I have laughed when they look so clever and talk about being on the <u>right</u> track. That joke about Leather Apron gave me real fits. I am down on whores and I shant quit ripping them till I do get buckled. Grand work the last job was. I gave the lady no time to squeal. How can they catch me now. I love my work and want to start again. You will soon hear of me with my funny little games. I saved some of the proper <u>red</u> stuff in a ginger beer bottle over the last job to*

write with but it went thick like glue and I cant use it. Red ink is fit enough I hope ha. ha. The next job I do I shall clip the ladys ears off and send to the police officers just for jolly wouldn't you. Keep this letter back till I do a bit more work, then give it out straight. My knife's so nice and sharp I want to get to work right away if I get a chance. Good Luck.

Yours truly

Jack the Ripper

Dont mind me giving the trade name

PS Wasnt good enough to post this before I got all the red ink off my hands curse it. No luck yet. They say I'm a doctor now. ha ha

Delivered to Scotland Yard, September 27, 1888.

CHAPTER 15
"It's never too late to mend..."

They don't make serial killers like they used to.

The 1960s were a "tough on crime" period in the United States. Civil rights marches were happening in cities across the country. Students were being shot and killed on their college campuses by their own government. Political conventions were marred by violence in the streets. War protests and tear gas were common sights on the evening news. Save for the rare Charles Manson, serial killers were laying low, and were relatively on their best behavior.

And then came the Supreme Court case Furman vs George in 1972 that declared the death penalty unconstitutional under the Eighth Amendment. If serial killers had a deterrent before, it was open game now.

For a nearly 20-year period, there were no executions in the United States. And suddenly there was a surge in serial killers. By the 1980s, they were making headlines throughout North America. Considering how rare executions were occurring, and how long it took for one to be carried out through court appeals, it is doubtful many serial killers bothered pausing. By the 1990s, executions began returning, and the number of serial killers began dwindling again. But the die had been cast.

And with it, came the 1992 spree of the I-70 killer.

Today, with executions back on the rise in many states, the question looms for serial killers: Is there a deterrent back in play?

In 1991, Emory Futo woke up in his California home, hopped on an airplane, flew to St. Louis, and went on a manhunt and killed his parents and two brothers one by one, then got back on a plane and flew home. Futo was sentenced to life in prison without parole. He had maintained his innocence for more than 30 years until he contacted me and said he wanted to tell his story. He confessed from his prison cell in Potosi, Missouri.

"I know now that what I did was wrong," Futo told me. "I hope and pray I will be forgiven. I'm sorry for all the pain I caused. I am so sorry. I know I am going to die in prison."

℀

Futo said he killed his parents because of years of physical and emotional abuse. He killed his brothers when they would not go along with his plan. As we talked, I asked Futo about whether the death penalty gave him pause or acted as a deterrent. "Never," he told me. "Never. I had gone through so much that once I decided I could not take it anymore, I knew what I had to do. I was so filled with rage and anger, nothing or nobody was going to stop me."

To be sure, there will always be serial killers stalking the streets, or in the case of the I-70 madman, stalking the interstate. FBI data says interstate killers fall into three distinct categories:

- Itinerant individuals who move from place to place.
- Homeless individuals who are transients.
- Individuals whose employment lends itself to interstate or transnational travel, such as truck drivers or those in military service.

The only one of those criteria that seems to fit the I-70 killer is the last one. Remember what Tim Relph said in Wichita. "I just do not see somebody just wandering between here and Indy without a reason. You have got to want to get here for something. Indy to Wichita is a long haul in two and a half days. I do not think he got in the car in Indy and decided 'I am going to go to Wichita and kill two people.' He did not have to come this far for this. You do not make that drive accidentally, especially branching off from Kansas City. Whatever happened in Indianapolis, this guy had to get on the road quickly to pull this off. He obviously traveled with a purpose. We just do not know what it was."

And FBI agents say with advancements in technology, the days of the serial killer may be numbered. "It is certainly a much more dangerous game for them today than it was during the time of the I-70 killer," said Ankrom. "When you consider the advancements of forensics and DNA, their chances of being caught are going to be much greater in the years ahead."

What has also changed are people's habits. We are all less vulnerable now with a cell phone in one pocket and perhaps pepper spray in the other. There are cameras everywhere waiting to snag a criminal in action. And when was the last time you saw a hitchhiker on the street with his thumb up?

"Bad guys used to have easy targets," says Ankrom. "Those days are long gone."

Most of us can look back on our youth where we walked along busy streets to school, or rode our bikes around town. Parents are having none of that these days.

"If we only knew then what we know now," laughed Detective Brad Rumsey.

Today, lethal injection is the most common form used by states for the killers who do receive the death penalty. Utah still has a firing squad on the books. They can still hang people in New Hampshire. And in the South, the electric chair is still in play.

But with many convicted murderers on death row for more than 20 years, it is much more likely the fear of being caught by modern technology is far greater than the fear of imminent punishment.

I found myself on the road, driving to Chicago, when Tim Relph popped into my mind, and his story of walking past the Otero home every day as a child, where nearly the entire family was murdered by Dennis Rader. And then I thought about Brad Rumsey, and the serial killers who had lived in his brain. And it suddenly hit me.

Joliet. Stateville.

The old Joliet, Illinois prison was to me what the Otero house was to Relph. I was a child when my family drove past it every week. I would stare at the block-long, giant sandstone walls, the guard towers on the upper corners, the silhouetted figures of trained snipers up there with their rifles pointed.

I may not have been able to get into the Herb Baumeister mansion, but I knew I could get into Stateville. I exited the highway and headed toward Joliet. The prison had been long closed, and was now a tourist site. It was built before the Civil War, just a few years after Joliet was founded. And like Alcatraz and some others, it was legendary among prisons. But the old Joliet prison that we called Stateville had its own specialty: This is where they sent the worst prisoners to die in the electric chair. And we were scared to death of the place.

From the 1920s until the 1960s, the electric chair was turned on 13 times at the old prison. Once, it was turned on 3 times in one day.

∾

I parked my car outside the prison and walked in. The main entrance is now a gift shop dominated by posters, T-shirts, and anything else you want of John Belushi and Dan Akroyd from the "Blues Brothers" film, where Joliet Jake Blues is released from prison and picked up by his blood brother Elwood in his Bluesmobile. They filmed the scene near the prison entrance here, with well-behaved prisoners in the background.

Greg Peerbolte greeted me upon my arrival. I told him I grew up scared to death of the old prison. "Well, if it makes you feel any better, 'Ghost Hunters' was just here filming a few weeks ago," he said with a big smile.

I stared at him. Then I asked, as nonchalantly as possible, "Did they find anything?"

Peerbolte laughed. "I don't know," he said, smiling again. "They seemed to leave in a hurry."

I started to leave too when Peerbolte hollered to me. "I grew up here too," he said. "Right down the street. Had to look at this prison every day."

I could not imagine.

"I was scared to death of the place," he said, smiling again. "Enjoy your visit."

I left the gift shop and walked into the yard. The prison had been closed for 20 years by then. Deteriorating buildings dominated the landscape. A cafeteria, library, laundry room, infirmary, gym, school, chapel, and warden's quarters were scattered throughout.

There was a long line of famous alumni at the old prison. George "Baby Face" Nelson called Joliet home, until it wasn't when he escaped. James Earl Ray slept here, doing time before getting out and killing Martin Luther King.

Joliet hosted the first mass murderer I remembered from my youth, Richard Speck, who tortured and killed eight women in the 1960s. Speck was sentenced to death in the Stateville chair, but when the Supreme Court threw out the death penalty, Speck spent the rest of his life here until his death in 1991. And he did not die quietly. A tape emerged of Speck wearing women's underwear, engaging in sexual activity with another inmate, snorting cocaine, flashing money, and bragging about living the good life in prison. "If they only knew how much fun I was having in here," Speck says on the tape, "they would turn me loose."

The wardens often had their hands full. In 1975, street gangs took over one of the cell blocks and held several corrections officers hostage. The warden at the time was a man named Fred Finkbeiner, who took to a bullhorn and promised the gangs they would not be punished if they would just let the officers go. Finkbeiner even sent in another gang member who agreed to help calm the storm. The rioting inmates murdered that guy.

As I looked out through the huge open spaces of the prison land, my mind went back to similar movie scenes. Burt Reynolds playing football in *The Longest Yard*, and Andy and Red talking in *Shawshank Redemption*. There was a baseball backstop on one side, some taken down basketball hoops on another.

I went into the jail cells. Bunk beds, toilet, sink. Untouched for 20 some years, they were falling apart now. But there was one in particular I was looking for, a special cell in a special building.

Death Row.

That building had about a dozen cells inside. It was always kept dark, with some cells also used to punish unruly inmates by sending them "into the hole" for segregation.

As soon as you enter the death row building, you see a large piece of artwork carved into the building's floor. "It's never too late to mend," it says. Perhaps for those in solitary confinement. But for those on Death Row, this was the witching hour.

This is where John Wayne Gacy spent his final days. Gacy is among the world's most notorious serial killers, having murdered 33 young boys near his Chicago home, burying most of them in the crawl space under his house. His conviction of those murders was the most homicide convictions in United States history.

As death day came calling for Gacy, he never gave anyone the satisfaction that death bothered him. A prison official said Gacy appeared normal and relaxed. He talked about the problems with the Chicago Cubs. His final meal was fried chicken and strawberries.

Outside the prison, people were chanting "Na na na na, hey hey hey, goodbye!"

When Gacy was strapped into his stretcher before the lethal injection, he declined to say anything. And then finally, in his last moment, he turned and mouthed some words. Those closest to him say he said, "Kiss my ass."

There was one final stop to make. I went back into the gift shop. "How much for that Blues Brothers shirt?" I asked.

"Which one?" the gentleman said as he pointed to dozens.

"The one that says, 'It's never too late to mend,'" I said.

I walked out of the prison and looked around. All those years in my memory were still there, but the building did not seem as large as it did in my youth. It was not quite as imposing. And I thought about Tim Relph and the Otero home. Time changes some things, but it cannot change everything.

CHAPTER 16

"If there is somebody who can listen to that tape and not be moved by it, they need to find another line of work..."

It was May 8, 1992, the day after Sarah Blessing was murdered in Raytown. There were now six bodies scattered along Interstate 70 between Indianapolis and Wichita. And everywhere along the highway, people were on high alert. Police detectives around the country kept watch and kept waiting. And the public kept watching and waiting with them. Alerts were put out to stores along the highways in Indiana, Missouri, and Kansas. Posters with composite sketches of the I-70 killer were put up everywhere. Newspapers throughout the Midwest had headlines screaming about the dangerous serial killer on the loose. Television stations ran pictures of body bags right next to the composite sketches on the evening news.

Police urged anyone and everyone with information to please come forward, and to please stop the killings.

And then they did stop, just as suddenly as they began.

Soon spring would turn to summer, then summer would turn to fall. A maniac serial killer who traveled the highway killing six people in less than a month had mysteriously gone quiet and dropped completely out of sight. Fall would turn to winter, then turn to spring again, and then summer again. There was no explanation. Police detectives throughout the Midwest were scratching their heads. They were thrilled the killings had stopped, but they needed more leads to catch their killer. Had the killer somehow fled the country, and if so, to where? Did he feel guilty about his crimes and decide to commit suicide? Was he in jail somewhere for some other crime? Did he somehow, incredibly, return to a normal life as if that murderous month in 1992 had never happened? Or, investigators pondered, did he meet his final fate in some other way, and was no longer alive?

September 25, 1993. Some five hundred days after Sarah Blessing was killed in Raytown, 51-year-old Mary Ann Glasscock went to work at her upscale Emporium Antiques store in Fort Worth, Texas, just off Interstate 35 and five hundred miles from Raytown. Around 11:30am, a repairman arrived at the antique store to do some planned work. He found a woman standing outside, who told him it appeared the store was closed and that there was nobody inside. The door was unlocked, and the repairman walked in. He discovered Glasscock's body in a pool of blood. Glasscock was older than the other I-70 murder victims, but everything else about her killing was eerily similar. Like the I-70 killings, Glasscock was a petite brunette, the small store sat in a strip mall area, and was just off an interstate. And like the I-70 killing scenes, Glasscock had been working alone, was shot execution style by a single bullet to the back of the head, there was little money missing, and an old residential neighborhood was behind the street. Like the I-70 scenes, a 22 shell casing was left lying on the floor. Unlike the previous murders the killer had left the victim partially nude and stole her car keys. It appeared the only thing of significant that really changed was the number on the Interstate, 70 to 35.

At the time Mary Glasscock was killed, Texas authorities were not initially aware of the I-70 investigation from a year earlier. There was no reason for it to be on their radar, hundreds of miles and now more than a year away. And, at first, it appeared their case, like the early I-70 killings, was simply another routine robbery turned homicide. That idea only lasted a few weeks.

On November 1, Amy Vess was working alone inside the small Dancer's Closet store in nearby Arlington, where children would go for their dance classes. A killer entered her store just before 6:30pm, ordered Vess to the back room, and shot her twice, once in the neck and once in the head. Again the similarities were striking. A petite brunette woman, working alone in a small store, just off

Interstate 35, ordered to the back and then shot in the head. This time there was $200 stolen, but the two Texas scenes seemed to resemble the I-70 killings in every other way possible.

Now authorities in Texas were talking to detectives in Indianapolis, Wichita, Terre Haute, St. Charles, and Raytown. To say those must have been stunning conversations would be an understatement.

Fall would turn to winter. And a killer was about to strike again, this time in Houston, and this time just off Interstate 69, near the loop that circles the city. Vicki Webb was working alone at her Alternatives Gift Shop when a man walked in, shot her in the head, and fled. He left Webb lying dead, but she miraculously survived. Vicki Webb had stared down her killer and would live to one day tell her story.

Texas police believed they now had their own Interstate serial killer on their hands. The question was, could it be the I-70 killer, did they have a copycat killer on their hands, or were the three Texas locations, despite their similarities, simply separate cases that stood on their own? Police departments throughout Texas and the Midwest began scrambling again, and got to know each other very well. Fort Worth police investigating the Mary Glasscock murder would call the similarities in Texas to the crime scenes along Interstate 70 "almost too similar to disregard." Arlington police working on the Amy Vess homicide said it was "definitely possible" the killer in

Texas was the same person, and they were looking into the I-70 killings. And when word of the scenes in Fort Worth, Arlington, and Houston got back to the homicide investigators in Indianapolis who were working the first of the I-70 murders, authorities there called the likelihood of the I-70 and I-35 cases being connected a "strong possibility."

But there was one very clear difference: The gun used in the I-70 killings was definitely not the gun used in Texas, as police discovered the ballistics did not match. There was no rare Erma Werke German Navy pistol being used in the Lonestar state. Perhaps there were indeed different killers. Or perhaps, as detectives soon came to realize, they made a serious mistake earlier in the investigation when they announced to the news media that they knew what gun the killer had used along the I-70 locations. If the I-70 killer and the I-35 killer were one in the same, all he had to do was switch guns.

And then suddenly, like in the Midwest, the killings stopped in Texas. This time, they appeared to stop permanently. And now, 30 years later, questions remain unanswered. Was he, or wasn't he? And if he was, why did he stop and then come back a little more than a year later? And what drove him to Texas?

Long time St. Charles Detective Pat McCarrick says trying to tie the I-70 killer to Texas is a very tough call. "I am the definition of the split decision," said McCarrick. "There are many people who are smarter than I am who believe that the I-70 cases and the I-35 cases are connected. And they may very well be. But I am not yet convinced that they are, but I am not yet convinced that they are not either."

The detective who has worked the I-70 case longer than any other is Mike Crooke. He inherited the first case in Indianapolis when Robin Fuldauer was slain and has followed it since, traveling around the country, speaking to various police agencies about it. Now, even in retirement, he is widely considered the leading authority on the I-70 killer. Crooke has traveled not just to all of the I-70 scenes, but also to the Emporium Antiques store in Fort Worth, the Dancer's Closet in nearby Arlington, and the Alternatives Gift shop in Houston. Nobody knows the lay of this land better than Mike Crooke.

"The similarities in all three of the Texas cases are just so close to what we were dealing with along Interstate 70," Crooke said. "It is just way too hard for me to ignore connecting them. You are more than welcome to call me crazy if you want to, but it is just a certain feeling that I had when I was at all the Texas scenes, that this has got to be connected to the I-70 killer. It is just a feeling that I have. I am not zeroed in and positive. But if they were connected, what was this guy doing between time periods?"

That time period was 16 months.

Could he have been in jail somewhere? In the military? Or simply back home somewhere, coaching a softball team and going to church?

There have been many times over the years, now over the decades, when one century flipped to another, sometimes when it is quiet, when Mike Crooke wonders if the I-70 case will ever be solved. When he has those moments, he pulls an old audio tape out of a drawer at home. The retired detective has gone over every piece of evidence countless times, but this piece is no ordinary piece. It will not solve the case, but it will motivate Mike Crooke forever.

It was November 1, 1993. The killer had just shot Amy Vess twice in Arlington, leaving her to die. But after the killer fled, Vess somehow summoned every piece of energy and courage she had left in her body and crawled on the floor to the store's counter, reached for the telephone, and called 911. She knew she was dying; she knew making that phone call would be the last thing she ever did. Barely able to speak, you can hear Vess choking on her dying breaths, barely able to speak into the phone.

"I have been shot," you hear Vess say, trying to spit out the words. The dispatcher asks Vess if she needs an ambulance. "Yes," Amy cries into the phone. The dispatcher then asks Vess if she knows where she is hurt. "In the neck," Amy says.

Crooke is overwhelmed every time he hears those words. "That tape will fire you up if you are having a time where maybe you are struggling and maybe you think you should just give up trying," Crooke says, his voice cracking as he recalls the tape. "That voice will get you chills every time you listen to it."

Meanwhile, hundreds of miles away, Pat McCarrick has the same tape in his drawer. And like Crooke, he also occasionally pulls it out to listen. He says you only need to hear it once. "How in the world did she even manage to get to the phone and complete the call?" McCarrick pondered as he shook his head. "It is such a terrible, terrible thing to listen to. People sometimes say to me 'Pat, you are spending too much time on this case. This case is cold.' Whenever I was told that by one of my bosses, I would go get that tape and play it for them. And I would only have to play it for them one time. After they hear it, they say, 'You know what Pat, you stay on that case.' If there is somebody who can listen to that tape and hear Amy Vess and not be moved by it, they need to find another line of work."

There is a horrible twist of fate in many of the killings. In Indianapolis, Robin Fuldauer was not supposed to be working on the day she was murdered. A co-worker called in sick. In Terre Haute, Michael McCown had a doctor's appointment that morning. He considered taking the rest of the day off, but decided to go to work. In St. Charles, Nancy Kitzmiller was supposed to be off that horrible Sunday afternoon. She agreed to work so a co-worker could have the day off. And in Houston, Amy Vess agreed to work that day, her day off. It ended with her calling 911.

And among the final heartbreaks was that Vess, like many of the other victims before her, still had a full life in front of her. Young and vibrant, Amy Vess was only 22 years old. She was still in college working part time as she headed into the real world. Instead, she met a killer.

CHAPTER 17
"You walk in on something like that, and it will stick with you forever..."

Police detectives up and down Interstate 70 were perplexed. Where was the killer? Did he have his fill? Did he kill himself? Maybe he was arrested for another crime and was sitting in a jailhouse somewhere. Perhaps he found love, got married, had a family, and began a new life. Everything was on the table.

Years would go by. A century would turn over. And then, out of the blue, word came from, of all places, Terre Haute again.

Less than a mile down the road from Sylvia's Ceramics store where Michael McCown was murdered sat the 7th & 70 Liquor Store on Prairieton Road. It was so close to Interstate 70 that you could see the store from the highway. And on the day after Thanksgiving in 2001, nearly 10 years after the I-70 killings, a man entered the liquor store around 6:30pm. By the time he walked out just minutes later, he had shot and killed Billy Brossman, who had been working behind the counter.

At first, it appeared to detectives to be a random, routine robbery gone bad. After all, Michael McCown, Sylvia's Ceramics, and 1992 was a long time ago. Police officers working now were not working then.

Brad Rumsey received the initial call. "I was the first responding officer on the Billy Brossman case in 2001," Rumsey said. "You walk in on something like that, and it will stick with you forever. But way back then I never thought that the Brossman case would turn into a cold case, and we had no reason to connect it to the I-70 case."

But then police discovered their gold mine: crystal clear store surveillance video with audio to boot. And what police saw shocked them. A killer that did not even bother to disguise himself, spoke into the camera, and barely took anything. "That video just made no sense," said Rumsey.

The surveillance tape showed the killer casually entering the store, walking to the back, grabbing a six pack of beer, then approaching the counter as if he was going to pay. He then quickly pulled a gun on Brossman and demanded the money in the cash register. Brossman immediately cooperated. The killer then grabbed a few bills, left the rest, and forced Brossman to walk to the back of the store, where he shot him once in the head, killing him instantly. The killer then ran quickly from the store, not even bothering to pick up the beer or the rest of the money in the cash register.

Detectives kept asking themselves, what killer decides to rob the store, then leaves the money behind? "He went into the store, grabbed some beer, and just left it," said Rumsey, shaking his head.

If his motive was not robbery, what could it possibly be? And as detectives investigated the Brossman case, they remembered the I-70 killer from a decade before, just down the street, who killed solely for the thrill of killing. They compared the surveillance video from the Brossman case to the I-70 killer composite sketches that sat in their files.

And the similarities were remarkable.

Besides matching the composite, the surveillance tape gave detectives other clues: they noticed the Brossman killer appeared to be wearing a wedding ring. And if you listen closely, you can hear the killer speaking as he pulls out his gun and orders Brossman to the back of the store. If the Brossman killer was indeed the I-70 killer, this was the first time they had heard his voice. But fingerprints left on both the beer and the cash register were too small for police to get a successful match.

Detectives knew someone somewhere would certainly recognize the suspect, so they decided to show the surveillance tape to the news media, and tips quickly began coming in. Terre Haute police had leads, but they could not get a confirmed match. And without a positive ID match, and without fingerprints, the Brossman case would remain unsolved. And any connection to the I-70 killer could only be classified as coincidental.

But for Brad Rumsey, it was never far from his mind.

More years would go by. More detectives would come and go. That Terre Haute case appeared to be another one gone cold. But police kept digging. They always felt that someone either knew the Brossman killer from the surveillance tape, or someone would eventually recognize him if they had not yet seen the tape. Eventually, they were proven right. Two people, claiming they recognized the suspect from the surveillance footage, eventually came forward. Both said they were nearly certain who the killer was. And it was not just the facial features they saw in the surveillance tape. What convinced them was the way the killer wore his pants. They were cuffed high. The killer they saw in the video looked exactly like the man they knew, and the man they knew always wore his cuffs very high. Ironically, for this identification, even a mask might have given the killer away. He may not have bothered to hide his face, but his real mistake was cuffing his jeans.

Police now had a solid lead, even if it was a strange one. And investigators later found other people who came forward with the same story. Looks like someone they know, they said. And yes, the cuffed pants. Police pressed and got a name, and they started digging. But the tips alone were not enough. They had to find the suspect. He was not in Terre Haute. He was not in Indiana. Eventually, they tracked him down and found him living in Missouri.

Terre Haute police began peppering him with questions. He told police he worked doing construction jobs for a large department store and traveled around the country doing remodeling jobs for their stores.

Had he ever done a job in Terre Haute, police asked.

Yes, the suspect said.

Any idea what year, police asked.

The suspect paused. Sometime in 2001, he said. When confronted with the details about the convenience store homicide, the suspect quickly denied that he had anything to do with the Brossman murder. He may have been in Terre Haute at the time, but he certainly did not kill anyone. The possible connection to the I-70 homicides was never brought up.

But Terre Haute police felt that with the surveillance video, the acquaintances who identified the suspect, and the fact that they could place him in Terre Haute during that time, they had enough to move forward in their investigation. Brad Rumsey wrote the arrest warrant himself. But prosecutors felt there was not enough evidence to move ahead with the case, and it was put on hold. Police needed more evidence to go forward. It still sits there today.

"That was a very tough pill to swallow," said one longtime Terre Haute detective who worked the Brossman case. "Very tough."

Frustrated, detectives were back to square one. But they never gave up on their suspect, and they never scratched him off their list for either the Brossman murder or the possible connection to the I-70 killings. There were just too many similarities to ignore. Striking in Terre Haute again; right off the highway again; walking the victim to the back of the store again; shooting the victim in the head again; killing apparently just for the thrill of killing again; walking out with little or no money again; surveillance tape pictures that matched the composite of the I-70 killer. No, Terre Haute police were not going to let this one become dust in the wind. It remains today in the front of their minds.

I asked Rumsey point blank if he thought the Brossman case was connected to the I-70 case. At that point, Rumsey's easy-going manner turned into a more guarded police-speak response. "It is unknown at this particular time if the Billy Brossman homicide is connected to the I-70 killer cases," said Rumsey. "But there are certainly some striking similarities. It is at least worth us looking at. But it would be premature to say absolutely yes, the Brossman case is part of the I-70 case. And we have developed some possible information on who that person is. But we are working on the Billy Brossman case completely separately from the I-70 case. Those two cases are not being worked in tandem. They are being investigated completely separately. But in our minds, there are definitely similarities. One day there might be a way we can connect the two cases. But at this point in time we cannot definitely do that."

Rumsey would not go any further, but I knew I had to find out how seriously Terre Haute police saw the connection, and how hard they pursued the two cases as being linked.

And I found out they tried hard. Very hard. And are still trying. Detectives from Terre Haute would meet with detectives from the other I-70 cities to compare their notes. They were briefed on Brossman. But until they could arrest someone in the Brossman case, there was never a reason to connect it to the 1992 rampage through the Midwest. Years would go by, but they kept trying. They would track the Brossman suspect down again, this time more than 15 years after the convenience store killing. They found him living in Texas, and this time they came with a warrant for his DNA. And that DNA sample still rests in a database today. More years have now gone by. But Terre Haute detectives are not giving up. Their Brossman suspect still sits at the top of their bulletin board. But they need more.

The I-70 serial killer case file sits on Rumsey's desk now as he prepares for retirement. And investigators have remained very cautious to publicly make any connection between the Brossman and I-70 cases. And thus, another horrific question still hangs in the balance: If the I-70 killer did indeed strike nearly 10 years later in a similar fashion, is it possible, or even likely, that he has struck somewhere else in the past 30 years? Not that detectives can find.

"No one has contacted our office about any other similar crimes like this," Rumsey said. "I have been reaching out to other agencies to see if they have any other cold cases that might be similar to ours. It is certainly something you have to look at. When you consider someone killing that many people in such a very short time span, then you have to worry that he might have continued to do so somewhere else at other times and maybe it has just somehow been missed."

Terre Haute detective Troy Davis is confident the two cases will eventually be solved. "You just keep working on these cases. We will not give up. I truly believe both the Brossman and the I-70 killings will be solved."

So the question remains: Could the I-70 serial killer have returned, nearly 10 years later, near the scene of one of his earlier killings, to kill again only once, just for the thrill of killing? Could he be the same man who killed Michael McCown down the street in Terre Haute, Robin Fuldauer in Indianapolis, Patricia Magers and Patricia Smith in Wichita, Nancy Kitzmiller in St. Charles, and Sarah Blessing in Raytown?

According to multiple police sources connected to both investigations, they believe the answer to that question is yes, he definitely could be. But "could" is not a word that goes far in homicide investigations.

And the chapter is not closed on the suspect, or the Billy Brossman investigation. As more years went by, detectives hoped other people would come forward. And just recently, one did. The witness was at one of the I-70 murder locations, and had just recently seen the convenience store video for the first time. The witness immediately picked up the phone and called police, telling them that they believed the person in the convenience store video is the same person they recall seeing at one of the I-70 locations. "Same height, same hair, same mannerisms, same complexion, same facial features," the witness told police.

I located the witness, who preferred to remain anonymous, and asked if they could estimate the age of the suspect they saw at the I-70 scene. "If I had to guess," the witness said, "the man I saw at the I-70 scene had a boyish, fresh look. He was probably in his late twenties."

Nearly ten years later, police estimate the man who killed Billy Brossman was in his late thirties. And the suspect police had been tracing all this time? He would have been in his mid- to late twenties at the time of the I-70 killings, and mid-thirties at the time of the Billy Brossman murder. A cold case was heating up again.

I called the witness back. "This is where the rubber meets the road," I told him. "I need to ask you point blank how confident you are that the Brossman killer is the I-70 killer."

The witness never paused. "Bob, I think it is him. I am pretty damn confident it is him."

After 30 long years, police had their best lead.

And in Terre Haute, it would fall in the lap of Brad Rumsey. The man who always knew he wanted to do this, the man who served his country, the man who walked in first to the Billy Brossman murder scene, the man who is chasing a serial killer, the man who is staring at a retirement date. "Plenty still left on my plate." Rumsey laughed.

CHAPTER 18
"You become a part of this. You just can't let it go…"

A man spends his life pursuing good versus evil, and then the day comes when it is time to walk away. But for some, it is an impossible task. Especially when the evil is possibly still lurking around the corner.

"I certainly do not think there have been too many days that have gone by that I have not given thought to the I-70 killer case," Mike Crooke says. "It is something that I am still hopeful that we will resolve some day."

Mike Crooke put on the Indianapolis Police Department badge on April 13, 1970. For nearly the next 50 years, he would be attached to a gun, a badge, a pager, and a police radio. He is retired now, but his thoughts often go back to that horrific day on Pendleton Pike, when death walked in and then out the front door.

It was the first of five stops for the I-70 serial killer. The Payless Shoe store on busy Pendleton Pike Road in Indianapolis. Robin Fuldauer would be the first of the six I-70 victims, shot in the head by a madman whose only motive appears to be killing for the sake of killing. The first officer on the scene at Payless that horrible afternoon was Crooke. He often has asked himself how different things would have been had that crime happened today, as opposed to thirty years ago.

"When I look back on the Robin Fuldauer case today, we did not have the advances in science, technology or DNA evidence that we have available to police detectives now. And as far as the media coverage goes, we did not have cable television or national network coverage back then. Those folks would have surely been out to cover this story, and all of the other subsequent killings along the highway. If this happened today, it would be national news for weeks. I have often wondered that if we would have had extensive, non-stop media coverage on these crimes from the very beginning, if we would have been able to come up with some better leads."

Crooke paused, and stated what is so obvious now, but was not in 1992. "Even something as simple as a security camera in these stores would have likely spared all of these lives."

Those early leads for Crooke in Indianapolis were very few and very far between because nothing made sense at the homicide scene. Murder in the middle of the day, in a very busy location, and yet no witnesses. Detectives were scratching their heads early in the Payless case. What was the motive? And three days later the bomb shell hit: A murder in Wichita, hundreds of miles away across the country, had the same ballistics as the gun that was used to kill Robin Fuldauer. It seemed impossible. But it was true. And when reality hit, it was Mike Crooke taking those phone calls.

Crooke can still remember what went through his mind nearly 30 years ago when he first heard about the Wichita murder, and then just weeks later when he heard about similar murders with the same gun in Terre Haute, St. Charles, and Raytown. Just like he still does today, Crooke went over all the possibilities in his mind, over and over and over again. "In the back of my mind, I still simply can't disregard any options on the I-70 case. It is such an outlier. Totally without explanations across the board. There are just so many holes. It is hard to make sense of anything the killer did."

Crooke agrees with Larry Ankrom and Tim Relph: the I-70 killer moved with a reason. "The killer clearly had to have had a purpose to go to these various places. Maybe it was something as simple as having relatives that might be living in the area. I just do not see him driving to these specific places just for the purpose of doing what he did. It makes absolutely no sense."

One of the first things that puzzled Crooke at the Payless store was how the killer was able to leave without being seen by anyone, and make his getaway. There was no one getting into any vehicle that anyone witnessed anywhere in sight. The only possible explanation is that the killer walked calmly out of the store and then away from the scene.

"We looked at everything," Crooke said. "Hitchhiking was the very first thought I had because he just disappeared into thin air, and nobody saw anybody get into a vehicle and leave. Then we asked ourselves, if he did have a vehicle, and it was not on site, where was it? Was it parked along the highway, where police could have come across it? Or a neighborhood where a resident would have seen him? We checked everywhere. But I do not believe that he could have parked a very long distance away. He had to get out of there, and quick."

The transportation question is so bizarre, it is within the realm of possibilities that the killer drove into the Speedway gas station, filled his tank, walked in and paid, then went next store and killed Robin Fuldauer before walking calmly back to his car and driving away. Who would have noticed?

Crooke said investigators early on looked specifically at military men, traveling salesmen and truck drivers.

And then there was the fact that five of the six bodies would end up in similar back room locations.

Like Ankrom, Crooke believed the killer was charming and easygoing, and convinced his victims that everything was going to be okay. "I think he was somehow able to persuade the victims that they were going to be just fine if they would just cooperate with him," Crooke said. "I think he put confidence in them that nothing bad was going to happen if they just did what he said, because there never was a sign of a struggle at any of these scenes. If you know you are about to be killed, you fight back. These people had no idea."

When the dust finally cleared after the Sarah Blessing murder in Raytown, and investigators realized they had a full blown serial killer on their hands, Crooke became the de facto go to authority on the case. He got in his car and drove to Terre Haute. Then to St. Charles. Then to Raytown. Then to Wichita. He wanted to see each of the crime scenes himself. When murders popped up a year later in Texas that were eerily similar to the I-70 scenes, Crooke went there too. Mike Crooke would leave no stone unturned. The I-70 case became known as the Crooke case. It still is.

"You go to a homicide scene, and you are never in your mind planning on something like a serial killer. It just shocks you. It is like 'oh my gosh, now what am I going to do?' Then you realize that you are no longer alone in the investigation. I now had four other police departments as partners now. I remember we had quite a number of people involved in the I-70 investigation. But I also remember that none of the investigators had ever dealt with anything like this before. This thing was new to everybody."

Crooke at first wondered why, traveling from Indiana to Kansas, then back to Indiana, then back through Missouri, the serial killer never stopped on his journey through Illinois, where he had to spend hours winding through Interstate 70. "When he left Indiana and traveled across I-70 toward St. Louis, why did he not stop somewhere else along the way? Is it possible he committed another crime somewhere else along I-70 in Illinois that we do not know about? There really was not much on Highway 70 in Illinois in 1992 once you pulled out of Terre Haute. It was not as built up like it is today. But still, that is a couple of hours through Illinois, back and forth, both after the first murder, and then again coming back after the second murder. Surely, he could have found some place to get off."

Just another unanswered question in a series of them.

Crooke remembers dealing with both Larry Ankrom and the FBI lab in Quantico to help develop a profile of the serial killer. "They were very intrigued with what happened to the killer in between the time of the killings. Was he changing the way he operated? Was he getting bored with the same thing? The profilers would tell us that serial killers often get incredibly excited when their act is completed. They told us it would not be uncommon for the killer to go to a hotel and crash for a day or two. They have fulfilled their fantasy. But where was he? We checked everywhere, all around the Midwest. He had to crash somewhere. But he was nowhere in sight." Hotel records checked up and down highways throughout the Midwest turned up empty.

Like investigators in the other I-70 cities, Crooke is hopeful that diligent detectives plus science and technology will help solve the case. And he has seen it before firsthand. In 1985, Crooke's first unsolved homicide case was 15-year-old Tracey Poindexter, whose body was found in a creek bed. Crooke kept a semen sample from the scene in the Indianapolis crime lab for years. The case went cold, but Crooke never forgot it. And as the years continued to roll by, DNA technology continued to grow. Sure enough, the DNA sample that Crooke stored away became relevant in 2001, and tied the murder to Terling Riggs, who was found guilty of the Poindexter murder.

"We can still solve this [I-70] case," he says, "I know we can. We have done it before."

Diligent detectives plus science and technology equals a chance at solving cold cases, no matter how old.

Now, thirty years later, back in Terre Haute, there is a new lead on the I-70 case. The 2001 homicide of convenience store clerk Billy Brossman, just down the street from the homicide of Michael McCown. "The Brossman case," said Crooke. "is certainly a very promising lead."

How good of a lead? "As good a lead as we have had in 30 years."

And now, many years after his retirement, Crooke is still the one that other officers working on the I-70 case reach out to when they have questions. To say he is revered among the other I-70 investigators is to put it mildly.

Crooke worked at the Indianapolis Police Department as a sergeant for nearly 40 years before moving down the road to Cumberland, Indiana, where he served as Police Chief for another 15 years before retiring in 2019. A life and career well served, with one very cold case still on his mind. And Crooke says he will see the case all the way until the end, even if it never ends.

Roger Spurgeon came to the Indianapolis Homicide Unit in 1976. "Mike [Crooke] was my trainer and my mentor," Spurgeon said. "He felt so strongly about new people getting the best exposure they could on investigating homicide cases. Mike always did his best to meet as many people as he could on a case, and then build and maintain relationships with them."

છ

I mentioned to Spurgeon that Crooke calls Susan Fuldauer every year on the anniversary of her sister Robin's death. "That is not surprising at all to me." Spurgeon smiled. "Mike does not need anything from her. But they both have a strong connection to Robin in ways that overlap. I believe it is therapeutic for both of them to have that relationship."

With Crooke retired, Spurgeon is in charge of the Robin Fuldauer investigation now. But that is only for official purposes. In the ultimate class act, Spurgeon informed Crooke that he could be the lead in the case for however long he wanted to be. "Mike has been a teacher, colleague, and friend," Spurgeon said. "I consider myself blessed to have had him in my life."

Crooke appreciates the gesture, and says he is on the I-70 pursuit to stay.

And the I-70 killer case will always be known as Mike Crooke's case. "They have given me the opportunity to stay involved in anything that is I-70 related. They have told me to remain the lead investigator for as long as I want to. And I definitely do want to."

Crooke says he misses the daily pursuit of cases like the I-70 killer, wants it solved desperately, and knows what the new police detectives who inherit such a case are up against. "Most of the new folks are absolutely fascinated with the twists and turns and the amount of work that police officers before them put into this case. And why wouldn't they be? This is one of those cases a lot of people would like to have a crack at solving."

And Crooke himself is still looking for answers. "I am still hopeful. I still think something will happen. If he is still around, we will eventually figure it out. If he is dead, maybe somebody will come forward."

And then, another twist hit the case. Between 1987 and 1989, three to five years before the I-70 killer struck, three female hotel clerks were murdered along Interstate 65 in Indiana and Kentucky. Now, some 35 years later,

DNA evidence tied Edward Greenwell to the killings. Greenwell died of cancer in 2013.

Back in St. Charles, Captain Raymond Floyd picked up the phone. "The time frame involved is just hard to ignore," Floyd said.

And there was something else. The composite sketch of the I-70 killer showed a lazy, droopy left eye.

Just like the one Greenwell had.

But there were also stark differences between Greenwell and the I-70 suspect. Greenwell was much older and taller. And while he robbed and sexually assaulted his victims, the I-70 killer did neither. Detectives working the Greenwell case said there was a "distinct possibility" that he killed more women elsewhere, but he never really fit the I-70 profile. And as the days and weeks moved forward, the task force, along with Indiana State police, did not believe Greenwell was connected to the I-70 murders.

Ↄↄ

Nobody sums up the frustration more than the first man on the scene, Mike Crooke. "You become a part of this," he said. "You just can't let it go."

Mike Crooke will enjoy his retirement. But understand, he will still have his fingers on the I-70 case.

CHAPTER 19
"We are not doing only saliva and semen tests anymore…"

The I-70 task force gathering at the Ameristar Casino was a tale of two worlds. Upstairs in a conference ballroom, police investigators from St. Charles, Indianapolis, Wichita, Terre Haute, and Raytown gathered in a large circle. The FBI and ATF were there. A DNA expert waited to speak to the group.

Downstairs, the dice were rolling, the wheels were spinning, the cards were dealing, and the drinks were flowing.

But back upstairs, where donuts and coffee surrounded the table, most of the people in the room were excited to hear about the latest DNA technology, what had changed over the years, and how the latest DNA methods might be able to help them solve this seemingly unsolvable crime.

At the time of the I-70 serial killer in 1992, forensic DNA analysis used a technology called restriction fragment length polymorphism (RFLP). But RFLP analysis required a very large quantity of DNA, and thus in many cases testing was unsuccessful or impossible. And if a DNA sample was compromised by environmental factors such as dirt or mold, RFLP analysis may again have been considered unsuccessful or unreliable. But newer DNA analysis enables laboratories to develop profiles from biological evidence invisible to the naked eye, such as skin cells. Today, valuable DNA evidence might be available that previously went undetected in earlier investigations.

Detectives sipped their coffee and waited anxiously. They all agreed that science and advancements in technology were their best chance to solve the 30-year-old case, bar someone coming forward with information or a suspect confessing. They were no longer holding their breath for either of those.

Jami Harmon looked around and surveyed the room. "You have to realize, things are just a lot different now than they were in 1992," she told them. "Start with time. It used to take us about six weeks or perhaps even longer to develop a profile from just one location on the DNA molecule. But In 1992, during the time around the I-70 homicides, there were advancements being made to get things done in 24 hours instead of six weeks and also getting six or seven locations on the DNA molecule instead of just one. DNA labs were switching from the older longer method to the newer faster method."

For hardened gumshoe detectives who learned their wares from hitting the pavement with notebooks in hand, they were learning there was a new game in town. And they liked it.

"In 1992," Harmon continued, "DNA testing locations across the country may all have been different. Some locations may have been more advanced than others. Today, labs are much more standardized. But the time around 1992 was becoming the infancy of what had been standard until today."

For example, in the St. Charles area where Nancy Kitzmiller was killed, a DNA testing lab did not open until 1998, six years after she was murdered.

And Harmon had more goodies waiting for the detectives. "Remember how one location on the DNA molecule advanced to six or seven around the time of this homicide? Today, we are able to look at 23 locations on the DNA molecule."

Harmon looked around the room. Detectives were taking notes and typing into their laptops. "But looking at more DNA makes the profile much more discriminating," Harmon warned them. "There are newer technologies out now. The whole genealogical element has been introduced, and that encompasses an entirely different type of DNA testing than what we are currently using as a standard."

And then Harmon gave them the words that were music to police detectives' ears from Wichita to Terre Haute. "Now, we are able to get what we call touch

DNA, or what we call handler DNA off of objects that we previously would not have been able to do in 1992."

In 1992 DNA testing was limited to semen and saliva. Detectives all knew there was no semen or saliva at any of their scenes. But touch DNA, with every item from every scene now suddenly in play? Could they find touch DNA, or handler DNA, on any of their items? Eyes lit up and smiles spread across the room. And the biggest smile belonged to Tim Relph, who kept the wedding veil. For the detectives, this was the home run. Whispers came from one to another as they began looking through their case files.

Harmon continued, "We are now able to take samples where skin cell DNA taken from someone that has handled something and use that sample to obtain DNA from those handled items," Harmon told them

Calls were made back to crime labs. Whatever they had, they would test again. What did they have? Where could they send it? How long would it take? They kept asking Harmon questions. She kept firing back answers. They were told to leave no stone unturned. They would send in everything they had. And then hope and pray on DNA results.

What, really, are the odds of solving a cold case, especially one that is 30 years old, with few witnesses and even fewer leads? They are not good. Yet it happens all the time, mainly thanks to the advancements in DNA that Harmond spoke about. Look no further than Indianapolis, where the I-70 serial killer began his murder spree.

In 2008, thanks to a federal grant, the Indianapolis Police Department established its Cold Case Division to attempt to solve older crimes through the use of DNA evidence. They began turning the clock back, all the way to 1977.

William "Billy" Wood had just turned 19 months old. He spent his days playing with his three-year-old sister Indy Jo. Billy's mother, Debra Shay, was at work, and left her children in the care of her boyfriend, Michael Ackerman. By the time police were called, Billy lay dead, suffering from multiple blunt injuries. Police questioned Ackerman. Indy Jo was too young for the police to interview. The testimony of a three-year-old would not have been allowed in court. Without enough evidence to tie Ackerman to the crime, Billy's death was ruled an accident. His mother and sister knew better.

Four decades after Billy died, and with only circumstantial evidence, the case, while still on the books, had long gone cold.

In 2008, Indy Jo was an adult. Having never forgotten about her little brother, she walked into the Indianapolis Police Department seeking answers, asking them to look at the cold case again. But the passing of years also meant the passing of witnesses, who died or disappeared. And there were other problems in a case so old. Records were lost. Memories had faded. Even the investigators still with the police department could barely even remember working the case.

And then Indy Jo found detective David Ellison. She couldn't tell her story when she was three, but she could tell it now. She said that when she was around eight, five years after Billy died, her recollections came back to that day. She said she remembered sitting with Billy at an orange and green child's table, one with a floral design, drinking grape juice. She then heard Billy screaming in the bathroom. She walked in there and saw Billy sitting on the sink with a purple face. Ackerman was shaking him by the shoulders. Indy Jo said she could not recall Ackerman hitting Billy, but insisted he was shaking him and was very violent with her brother.

Ellison went forward, determined. The Indianapolis Police Department built a case against Ackerman. He was charged and convicted of murder.

David Ellison was far from finished. In 1989, 16-year-old Amy Weidner was raped and murdered. The case quickly went cold. More than twenty years went by. Ellison went back over the case files, re-examined old evidence, and talked again to several witnesses. He found a palm print from the scene. But DNA was in its early stages in 1989, and there was no match.

In 2002 Ellison, Roger Spurgeon, and Sergeant William Carter teamed up to look over their cold cases. Incredibly, they had 800 of them. They were all needles in the haystack. Police take all sorts of tips, and in the Weidner case, they took one from a man who said he had visions of the murder in a dream. Another 10 years went by. Advancements were made in DNA. Carter began contacting all of Weidner's friends from nearly 25 years before, seeking DNA samples that might match their print. A new name popped up that had not been interviewed years ago: Rodney Denk. Police arranged to meet with Denk, but he failed to show up. They went looking. Denk had an arrest record with a palm print. Police sent it in and waited for a possible DNA match. It came back positive. When police tracked him down, Denk pulled a knife and tried to cut himself.

Where did police get Denk's name? He signed the guest book at Weidner's funeral. He would later admit to the murder, saying he was a friend of Weidner's brother, went to their house to burglarize it, only to find Amy there. Denk pleaded guilty and was sentenced to 65 years in prison.

They were just getting started solving some of those 800 cold cases in Indy.

In 1999, 83-year-old Victor Gregg's body was found in his garage, covered with blood. He had been strangled to death. Gregg was a World War II veteran. Police had Gregg's blood-stained clothes and a keychain. But there were no witnesses, and the case went unsolved for years. Until the detectives started looking at their files again. Police initially believed blood evidence from the scene was Gregg's. But as DNA technology advanced over the years, it became apparent that the blood was not his. Police started searching databases, and found the blood at the scene actually matched a person that was already in the DNA database. His name was Frank Tiller, who had previously been charged with another crime in Louisiana. David Ellison headed south to search for Tiller. Detectives found him, got a DNA swab sample, and it matched the scene. He was arrested and found guilty of murder. Do not tell David Ellison or the homicide unit in Indianapolis that they cannot solve a cold case.

And it is not just Indianapolis. And it does not matter how far detectives have to go back to solve a crime, and it does not matter what they have to do to solve it.

Consider Detective Brad Rumsey in Terre Haute. Turn the clock all the way back to 1967. Thirty-two-year-old Jo Ann Fox, mother of two, had just moved into the Manor Apartments, a boarding house. On her first night there, police discovered her body. She had been raped and beaten over the head with a soda bottle. There was never an arrest, and the world had not yet heard of DNA. Fifty years went by, and in 2018, Fox's children knocked on the Terre Haute Police Department's door. Could they reopen their mother's case, after all these years, and take another look at it? Problem was, nobody working at the Terre Haute Police Department in 2018 had ever heard of the case from 1967. Most people there were not even alive at the time. Police Chief Shawn Keen went deep into the building's basement, turned on the lights, and started combing through boxes. And there he found one marked "old stuff." Inside was the file of the Jo Ann Fox case.

This landed on the desk of Rumsey, who began digging, and try to track down witnesses from 51 years ago. Anyone in Fox's age bracket at the time of her murder would be pushing 90 now, if even still alive. Not only was it a cold case, it was a cold chase.

Finally, Rumsey found a person of interest he wanted to talk to. The man now lived in Sarasota, Florida. With a DNA kit in hand, Rumsey hopped on an airplane. He returned with a sample. The man, 76 years old now, was 22 at the time of Fox's murder. Rumsey's work was just beginning. Now he needed a DNA sample from Fox. That meant exhuming her body in 2021, 54 years after she was buried. Her family agreed. Rumsey handled the scene, and police await results.

There is a memo to killers: No matter who you are, where you are, and how many years you have gotten away with the crime, detectives are still on your tail.

The same ones that are on the tail of the I-70 killer. They have been successful before, and they can be successful again.

CHAPTER 20
"We can get DNA from just one and a half skin cells…"

As the task force headed back to their respective cities, they realized they had one lead above all others: the Billy Brossman case in Terre Haute from 2001. Similar killing, just down the street from the I-70 killing of Mike McCown, surveillance pictures, and possible DNA evidence from inside the convenience store. Terre Haute would quickly become the focus of the I-70 investigation. The rush was on to send DNA samples from the McCown case to labs to see if they could possibly match up with the Brossman case.

Detective Rumsey in Terre Haute reached out to DNA Labs International in Florida, the second largest private lab company in America, handling only homicide cases, with a specialty in cold cases. "Cold cases are our passion," said Allison Nunez, Laboratory Director and Chief Operating Officer of DNA Labs.

And DNA is no longer the only catch phrase. Intelligence, Hair Shaft testing, STR, Y-STR, and M-Vac collection are all part of the DNA game now. The lab recently extracted DNA from the nails of an unidentified female from nearly 100 years ago, something that would have been unheard of not long ago.

☙

The technology that police agencies around the country dream of is sitting in the offices of testing facilities like DNA Labs International. They can sometimes return results in 24-48 hours, although most cold cases, like the I-70 killer, usually take a couple of months. They have a database with more than 65,000 DNA profiles.

Still, in many cases, and the I-70 case is certainly one, there is either no DNA, insufficient DNA, or degraded over time DNA. It just makes the testing that much harder.

Remember what long-time Detective Pat McCarrick of St. Charles said: "We just need a name. If we can get a name, we can put a case on a guy."

For example, look at gun evidence. With new technology, DNA Labs International has an 85% success mark with DNA samples involving guns, specializing in spent shell casings or fingernail DNA, sometimes involving only one shell casing left at the scene. Of course, the I-70 cases are littered with shell casings left behind. "Shell casings specifically are our specialty," Nunez said. "We can do shell case technology that no one else can. Four or five years ago, our success rate for shell cases was around 5 percent. Now it is around 40 percent and growing."

In many cases, evidence at crime scenes results in very limited amounts of DNA, and thus would not yield enough DNA for a sample. Enter the new world of forensic genetic genealogy. The technology that was previously used for tracing family ancestry is now being used to solve cold cases. Investigators can now build out family trees using DNA databases. Forensic genealogy can now often provide labs and police agencies with new leads, even if there is no direct DNA match. It is night and day compared to 30 years ago.

"You look at the I-70 case from 1992," Nunez says, "and we would have needed a lot of blood back then to solve the case. Now, we can get DNA from just one and a half skin cells."

And now, there is nuclear DNA. It is obtained from rootless hair shafts, needing just a one-sixth centimeter size piece of hair.

"We are constantly training police departments about what is new," Nunez said. "It really is a team effort to get these cases solved…. We are constantly asking why," Nunez said. "Cold cases like the I-70 killer take longer to solve. We work in tandem with police departments around the country, going through every report, every piece of evidence. A lot of what we do is reviewing the case ahead of time, to be ready when the final report comes."

In a case like the I-70 killer, which did not yield a DNA profile or suspect earlier, DNA technology has moved to what is called the "wet vacuum collection technique," where items such as clothing and porous metals near the crime scenes are now processed. These could include things like rocks and bricks, or samples from large surface areas.

And it was the clothing that became the key in the Michael McCown case from Terre Haute. Remember, this was the only scene where police could verify something was clearly missing: McCown's wallet. And 30 years later, police still have his pants from that day. If his murderer reached into those pants to grab the wallet after he shot McCown, those pants might hold the key to touch or handler DNA, and the "wet vacuum collection technique" would hold the key to the Terre Haute testing.

As Terre Haute and the task force anxiously waited for their results, they knew the odds were still stacked against them. Thirty years is a long time. They had sent other samples off for testing before. But there was clearly hope that this time, thanks to technology, it might be different.

Even positive DNA results can only take you so far, but negative results do not mean the end of the line. Nunez emphasizes that being excluded in one DNA match does not mean a killer is excluded from other crime scenes. And it does not mean that the police agencies working a case along with the labs will ever stop hunting. "[Finding that killer] is the goal," Nunez said. "That is why we do this."

And they have been successful.

In Georgia, results from the lab recently brought murder charges in a 33-year-old cold case. In Washington, a 28-year-old cold case landed a suspect who had been deceased for years. And in Florida, a 40-year-old case was solved, after the suspect had been dead for 25 years.

So yes, it is possible, no matter how long it takes.

With all of the officers now looking in their evidence closets for possible DNA opportunities, the focus shifts back to the task force, and its headquarters in St. Charles, where a changing of the guard was taking place with Kelly Rhodes taking over the Nancy Kitzmiller case. For Rhodes, this was a position she never dreamed of being in. Not in a million years.

Rhodes was born just after the Interstate 70 serial killer terrorized the Midwest. Growing up in the Lake of the Ozarks area, she was far removed from the highway, and had not heard much about the case until she took a job with the St. Charles Police Department a few years ago. Rhodes quickly began moving up the ladder into the detective ranks. When Stepp, who has handled the Nancy Kitzmiller investigation for years, decided it was time to retire, it surprised no one but Rhodes herself that she was chosen to take over the case. "I certainly never expected this," she said.

And she has thrown herself into the case. Every minute. Every day. Her desk has been cleared of other duties. Kelly Rhodes, like Don Stepp before her, is now the face chasing the madman in St. Charles.

When Rhodes turns the lights on in her office, she stares at 30 years of files. "This is not the kind of case that you see every day." Rhodes laughed.

Rhodes is literally going through thousands of pages, organizing everything into her own system, not just learning everything possible about the case, but also looking for that special hidden needle in the haystack. "This is a very, very big case," she said. "You want to make sure that nothing has been missed."

Rhodes understands being the lead in St. Charles can be daunting. But she is ready. "I was very excited when they asked me to do this," Rhodes said. "The previous investigators have set us up for success with the new technology that we have now to bring this case to a close. I feel really good about this."

Like everyone else, Rhodes says she is amazed when she looks at the I-70 case. "There just does not seem to be any motivation for these crimes. Even the money taken was very minimal, so it does not even appear that robbery was a motive. We have no answers and no reasons why."

That does not mean that they will not one day find one.

"It has been many years since they have collectively taken a good look at this case," Rhodes said.

Rhodes knows she is not alone. Like Pat McCarrick and Don Stepp before her, she has partners now in Indianapolis, Wichita, Terre Haute, and Raytown. There are brains to be picked, especially the ones that went before her. "I am so fortunate to still have Pat and Don out there," Rhodes said.

Meanwhile, as the calendar turned, Stepp kept putting off his retirement. You do not even have to ask him why he can't just "step" away like he had planned. "It would be very important to the Kitzmiller family," Stepp said. "I do not think anyone would ever want to be in that place that the Kitzmillers are in. It is not something that just ends with time. It is always going to be there for the rest of their lives. I believe these families have paid enough. I believe it is time they are all rewarded with an answer. They all deserve it."

Stepp desperately wants to see where the I-70 case goes. "Technology has changed so much in 30 years," he says.

And Don Stepp would know. It was June 2007 when Bob Eidman went to work at his Brooke Auto Insurance Company, which he owned, in St. Charles. Minutes later, he was shot to death in broad daylight. A post office worker would discover his bullet riddled body. Only Eidman's wallet had been taken. St. Charles police found both live ammunition and shell casings at the murder scene. Police also had a surveillance tape from a business next door to the insurance company that showed a white Ford

Focus pull up in front of Eidman's business just before the shooting, and then quickly leave afterwards. A gold mine for police. So they had clues. But despite their evidence, and their potential list of suspects from family and friends, the case quickly went cold. Three years passed.

What police still had was Eidman's jacket, where he kept his wallet. And then they ventured into the new world of touch DNA. And they got a hit. The DNA matched a man named Paul White who was already in prison. When St. Charles detectives tracked White down, they discovered he was a customer of Eidman's. And they quickly discovered that White was once a passenger in a vehicle driven by a man named Cleo Hines that had been stopped in a previous traffic matter. That vehicle was a white Ford Focus.

White denied he had anything to do with the Eidman murder. But when police found Cleo Hines, he told a much different story. He told police that White had lost more than $1,000 at the casino the night before Eidman was killed, he told Hines he knew Eidman kept cash at his office, and he forced Hines at gunpoint to drive him there. In 2012, White was found guilty of murdering Eidman, and sentenced to two life terms. Without advancements in DNA technology, police would likely have never solved the case.

And one of the lead detectives on that case was Don Stepp, who never stops thinking about DNA, science, and technology, and what they have meant in solving murder cases over the years.

Stepp can walk away now with his head held high. He has fought the good fight, not just on the Nancy Kitzmiller or Bob Eidman cases, but on all of the others as well. A proud marine who joined the police force because he wanted to be part of something big, something with teamwork and camaraderie. Now, there is a fishing pole, a lounge chair, and a cold drink waiting for Stepp after a job well done. "I will still be around if they need me." He laughed.

Because there is a much bigger fish to catch.

CHAPTER 21

"Miss Webb, are you the woman I am looking for?" Another pause. And then, "I probably am..."

There was one person among all others that I needed to find. Every police detective, every grieving family member, and every witness was vital to me. But the big fish in the pond was a long way away from Interstate 70. Vicki Webb had miraculously survived an assassin's bullet. Was it the I-70 killer's? The gun was different in Texas, but everything else was the same. Young woman, working alone, small store in a strip mall, right off the Interstate, middle of the day, no robbery, no sexual assault, no nothing. Just the thrill of the kill. Only the name of the highway had changed.

⁀

One year after the I-70 killings, the scene moved to Texas. Two women in the Dallas area were killed in similar incidents. And then a third scene, in Houston, where Vicki Webb was shot and left for dead but survived.

Thirty years had passed. Where was she?

I quickly found out she was not in Houston. In fact, she was nowhere to be found. I started with the Houston Police Department. "Good luck," I was told. "Vicki Webb disappeared a long time ago."

I kept calling. Other area police departments, news organizations, chambers of commerce. Nothing. Webb, understandably, had gone into hiding long ago.

With only a name and an age, I checked marriage and divorce records. The search narrowed, but still seemed impossible. Nobody in the task force knew of her whereabouts. "If you find her," one detective laughed, "send her our way."

I knew that I had to find her. And there was only one way: the old-fashioned way. "Hello, I am sorry to bother you, my name is Bob and I am looking for the Vicki Webb who was shot 30 years ago in Houston."

"Who? What? Who are you?" Click.

Many of those random phone calls did not go well. It is an uncomfortable part of the journalism business. And I still had more than a thousand Vicki Webb's out there, if she still even had the same name, which I doubted she did.

I received a couple of potential leads from police sources, and narrowed my search. An FBI source said he heard she remarried, moved out of state far away, and kept moving again, from state to state. "This happens when a man who tries to murder you learns later that you are still alive," he said.

Vicki Webb made herself nearly impossible to find. I kept making awkward calls. Weeks went by, and still nothing. And then...

"Hello, I am sorry to bother you, my name is Bob, I am a news reporter, and I am looking for the Vicki Webb who was shot 30 years ago in Houston."

There was a long pause.

"Hi," a soft, quiet voice on the other end said. That was far from the response I usually got.

"Miss Webb, are you the Vicki Webb I am looking for?"

Another pause. And then...

"I probably am."

And with that came an incredible sense of relief. But I was only halfway home. I told her that I was working with the task force, and they were going after the I-70 killer one more time, 30 years later. "Can we talk?" I asked her. "On the record. Can you tell me your story?"

There was obvious concern on Webb's end. Talking publicly would be the opposite of what she had been doing for 30 years. "I don't know," she said. "I would like to help in any way I can, but I just do not know."

I made it clear to her that I would not pressure her, anything she did would be on her terms, and I asked her to take some time and think about it. She promised to keep in touch. We had numerous phone and text conversations over the next few weeks. We talked about the task force, about the advancements in DNA technologies, and about whether police thought her assailant was indeed the I-70 killer. She was interested in the places I had already visited, and the families and witnesses I had already met. And she was intrigued by the Billy Brossman case.

I knew she wanted to talk, but it was a big step for her, and I certainly respected that. She told me she would have an answer for me in a couple of days.

A few days later my phone rang. It was Vicki.

"Hello young lady," I said, fingers crossed.

"Bob Cyphers," she said excitedly into the phone, "let's do this!"

And now I paused. "Are you sure?" I asked. "I would completely understand if you were not comfortable with me or this."

"I am sure," she answered. "I want to catch this guy. I have had enough of him haunting my life."

We kept talking. When could we do this? Where could we meet? Was anything off limits?

"I'm ready," Webb said. "The sooner the better. I will fly to you. Nothing off limits."

Sometimes you can picture people before you meet them. Sometimes you are right. This time, I could not have been more wrong. I had pictured a somewhat older woman, probably a bit frail, a bit concerned about coming forward, clearly nervous about where the interview might go. I was wrong on all counts.

"I am so ready for this," Vicki Webb said as we shook hands. "Let's do it."

"Just start at the beginning," I told her. "Take your time. I am not going anywhere."

And then this incredible, strong woman sat down and began telling her incredible story. For the next several minutes I just sat and listened.

CHAPTER 22
"I will always say he looked like a horse racing jockey…"

It was a crisp winter Saturday morning, and Vicki Webb had only one thing on her mind: it was definitely time to get away. "My day started out wonderfully. I was going on vacation!" Webb remembered.

But before she could hop on a plane, Webb had one more day of work at her Alternatives Gift Shop, a small little store in the Rice Village shopping district near Rice University, where students were just coming back to campus from their winter break. It was less than a mile south of Highway 69 in Houston.

Vicki Webb said she was unaware of the I-70 killings happening across the country nearly two years earlier, or the murders of Mary Ann Glassock and Amy Vess in the Dallas area just a few months prior. Small shops, just off the interstate, six locations now, eight body bags, all women working alone except one.

Vicki said she opened her store at 10am, and was working alone. One of her first customers that morning was a short man with long, shaggy blond hair. Vicki said she recalled him wearing a beige, old time cardigan button up sweater. She remembered that he walked sort of bow legged. She said the man spent a few minutes just looking around the store, and she had no reason to think he was anything but a customer browsing for some items like everyone else.

Of course, he was not.

"I remember noticing right away that he was a rather short guy," Vicki said. "He was definitely under six feet tall. Maybe he was around five feet, eight inches tall or so. He was rather thin. I would describe him as very gaunt, and very skinny. I will always say he looked like a horse racing jockey. That is what I keep coming back to."

He appeared like every other customer. Just another next-door neighbor doing some shopping on a Saturday morning.

Of course, he was not.

"He just walked into the store and really just started looking around and then he started talking to me," Webb said.

Now, 30 years later, Webb can still see the man in her dreams. "I would guess he was probably in his mid-30s.

He could have been a bit younger. He was very tanned and he had a very leathery or weathered look. A worn-down look. I still keep thinking, 'this man has to have worked somewhere outside.'"

Vicki Webb's date with destiny was just minutes around the corner.

And the man kept looking, and the two of them kept talking. "He kept asking me several questions about traffic in the area around the store," she remembered. "He wanted to know if I got a lot of walk-in traffic at the store. I said, 'Well, I am a very small gift store and it is the middle of January.'"

Webb said she found it a bit odd that the man was hanging around, but she kept talking to him. What else could she do? She noted that the customer appeared more interested in the area around the store than the items inside it.

"I was talking to him very much like a business person would, thinking, 'Oh this gentleman is looking for real estate or something in the area.'"

Of course, he was not.

And then a car pulled in front of the store next to Webb's. And soon another customer walked into her store. Things were getting busy in the area around Rice Village, and the customer chatting up Vicki Webb decided to leave. "I will be back in a couple of minutes," he told Webb.

"I found that kind of odd. He was acting very strange," Vicki said. "Who could think anything else besides this is a strange guy? I just assumed he was another customer."

Of course, he was not.

The new customer in the store left, and sure enough, the first customer kept his promise and returned right away. "He then started telling me that he was waiting to meet his niece," she said. "He kept telling me how much his niece would like my store."

Vicki noticed the man kept looking out the store's front window. She assumed he was looking for his niece to arrive.

Of course, he was not.

They kept talking.

"He was acting like he was in the same kind of business as me," Vicki said.

The customer was in the store the second time for roughly 15 to 20 minutes. "He was looking out both sets of windows toward the parking lot," Vicki said. "He kept mentioning his niece."

The man would occasionally leave the windows and look around the store, as if he was shopping for something.

Of course, he was not.

"He was very pensive," she said. "He never really got very close to me. But he was acting very nervous. But I was closing at 4pm and going on vacation! My mind was certainly not there."

The man then pointed to an item that he said he wanted to see. "He said something about a copper picture frame that he wanted to look at," Vicki said. "He pointed at the wall where the frame was. I walked over to where it was and pulled it down. I then handed it to him and then I turned around to go behind the counter to ring up the sale. Everything seemed like he was going to pay for the frame."

Of course, he was not.

And then time stood still for Vicki Webb. In a flash, Her assailant struck. "I never heard him come up on me. I never heard a thing. I never saw a gun. I just heard a loud pop behind me." But Webb knew something had happened. She just did not know what.

"I realized I was falling very slowly down. I fell on my right-hand side. My mind had not quite registered what had happened at that point."

The customer had shot her in the back of the neck. Vicki fell to the floor, still conscious but not able to move. "I just remember laying there on the floor and thinking 'oh my gosh, I am in big trouble.'"

The customer then jumped over the counter and grabbed less than $100 from the cash register.

"All I could see was his feet. But I will never forget them. He had on brown cowboy roper boots."

She lay on the floor, bleeding and wondering what was next. All she could do was listen. "He went to a small room in the back of the store and opened the door. It was my storage closet. It was packed with all of my stuff. There was no room in there for him to do anything. He closed it and then came back over to where I was laying."

She did not know it yet, but she was paralyzed. She remembers that she could barely breathe. "My breathing was so shallow he would not have been able to detect it anyway."

Vicki says her mind focused on one thing: staying alive. "I thought, 'oh God, please do not take me just yet. I have a 13-year-old daughter to raise.'"

Vicki knew her only chance to stay alive was to play dead, and hope the shooter thought he had killed her. Her mind raced at how to play dead. "I remembered watching those old movies on television. One time, when I was a kid, I almost drowned once, but I remembered a movie with Burt Reynolds, where he swam sideways to survive, so I remembered it and I swam sideways that day and I did not die."

She laughed at the memory. The old movies saved her once. Could they do it again? "I always remember watching movies after someone has been shot, and they always struggle trying to get up, and I always think, 'Oh you idiot, you are telling this person you are not dead! This person clearly wants you dead!' So I told myself at that moment, 'You are not some kind of idiot, Vicki Webb. You will just absolutely lay there and just pretend to be dead.'"

Vicki says she could not feel anything and was still having trouble breathing. But she was able to breathe a big sigh of relief when the shooter fled from the store. But that feeling soon turned to absolute horror when she heard him return moments later. "I just kept my eyes closed and prayed," she said. "I knew this horrible individual wanted me dead. Why, I did not know. But for some reason, this person wanted me dead."

But he was back now, perhaps uncertain if he had finished the job, and soon he was rolling Vicki over and dragging her behind the counter. "He jumped back over me. He pulled my legs down. I was now lying flat. He apparently took my trousers off, which I did not remember at the time. But police say he did. But I was not raped."

And then Vicki, eyes closed and barely breathing, waited and wondered what would happen next, and how much longer she might have to live.

She did not have to wait very long.

"He put the gun back to my forehead," she said before pausing. "And then he pulled the trigger again."

There are moments in all of our lives that we look back on. For Vicki Webb, on a day that began with her looking forward to a warm beach, a man shooting her and leaving her for dead would be remembered forever. But when she breaks down that day, it comes back to the second time her assailant pulled the trigger.

Vicki paused again, and her words came out slowly. "And It just went click..."

Time stood still. The gun had jammed. "Then he just laughed," she said. "He thought that was funny and he just laughed. He is a very sick man."

Vicki said she then heard some noises coming from outside her store. Her attacker must have heard them too, and he quickly fled for the second time. "He was only there to kill whoever happened to be there," she said. "And it happened to be me."

Vicki says she would lay on the floor, in her blood, unable to move and barely able to breathe, for about 10 to 15 minutes. She listened to the noise of shoppers outside.

Suddenly, she heard the tinkling sound of the bell attached to the store's front door. A couple had arrived in her store to shop. Webb could hear their voices, but she could not see their faces. "I said to them, very weakly, 'Excuse me. Can you please get me some help? I have been shot.'" With her eyes now open, Vicki lay on the floor, thoughts of what had just happened racing through her mind. "The things that go through your head, there is no way that I can explain. They make absolutely no sense whatsoever." She laughed again.

"I remember thinking, I can't move my arm. Did he saw off my arm?"

And then she had hope. "It is funny, because immediately, I felt okay," Webb said. "I knew that I had been shot, but I also knew I was going to be just fine. I never lost consciousness the entire time. I had not one ounce of pain until the door dinged and the couple came in. And then it was excruciating."

And then the ambulance arrived. "I remember the ambulance man helping me, saying, 'We are only about 5 minutes away, but this is going to be the longest ride of your life.' He was right about that."

Every stop and start. Every bump in the road. It was like she was being shot all over again. By the time she arrived at the hospital, the pain got worse. Much worse. "If you are a female, and you had a child, to me that pain level is about a three at the worst and I have had a child. But this was absolutely unbearable."

Webb's head could not be touched. "My head was hypersensitive. You could barely touch a hair on my head, and I would scream. It was an indescribable pain. I did not wish to live if I was going to stay like that. My head felt like an ice pick with an electric current running through it."

Then Vicki and I took a break and went to lunch. There was so much more I needed to ask her, and then I realized I did not have to. She was pouring it out. All I had to do was listen.

CHAPTER 23

"That man took a lot of my life away from me. And once I made the choice that he could not have any more of it, I have never looked back..."

I watched in awe as Vicki Webb picked at her salad. We talked about her life after the shooting, her family, and her decision to talk. I wondered if I could be that strong in a similar situation. In a word, after a life sheltered, she was now fearless.

In the days after the shooting, Vicki Webb lay in a hospital bed fighting for her life. Her mind never drifted far from that day, her store, a man who pretended to be shopping before he left her for dead. And the vacation that never happened.

A bullet was still lodged in her body. Doctors were scrambling. And her family was convinced she was going to die. But Vicki insisted that she knew better, that she knew her body, and that eventually everything was going to be just fine. But the only person who believed that was Vicki Webb. "I could have put all of them at ease if they would have just listened to me," Vicki said. "Because I knew that at some point I was going to be just fine. Certainly not right then I was not. But there was never any doubt in my mind that I was going to make it. I just did not know how long it would take."

She says she only survived thanks to an extremely rare spinal abnormality that caused the assailant's bullet to ricochet off her vertebrae and then lodge in her head. Today, she can laugh about it. "I am only here today because I have a ridiculously abnormally large spinal column," she said. "Where this guy shot me, a million other people would have been dead on the spot."

The bullet struck her somewhere in between her second and third vertebrae. It then chipped a bone that wound up striking her spinal cord, leaving her paralyzed from the neck down, and surgeons were not able to find an easy way to remove the bullet from her spinal column without causing problems elsewhere.

"I did have many touch and go moments in the hospital," Webb remembered. "The doctors really wanted to do surgery to get the bullet out, but they said I might lose the use of my right arm. I thought about it for a second or two and then I told them, 'Let's keep the bullet in, I am good.'" Police detectives, of course, would like that bullet to check for ballistics. But Vicki Webb has sole possession of it. Nearly 30 years later, the bullet still rests in her neck. and she insists that is where it will stay. "It is mine forever," she says. "It has become a part of me."

Even with all the pain and side effects. "Yes, I still feel the effects of the bullet every single day of my life. I would not really describe it as pain, but more sort of an uncomforting feeling. What I really feel on a daily basis every day is that somebody is choking me! It is my new normal now. I ache every single day of my life."

Webb would eventually undergo multiple surgeries to address her paralysis. And after those surgeries came three months of rehabilitation. And then Vicki Webb was finally able to walk again. The only evidence that any crime was ever inflicted on her body is the bullet that is still lodged in her neck.

"I have always considered myself a very independent individual, and I immediately went on to becoming a very dependent individual," Vicki said. "I lost three months of my life because of that man and that horrible day. You have to learn to do everything over again when you are paralyzed. You are literally starting over from scratch."

After the shooting she was obviously worried. She decided to lay low, and avoided any publicity surrounding the case. Fear always hung in the air. Did the gunman know she was still alive? Might he try to track her down? Webb remarried, changed her name, and moved out of state, far from the bright lights of Houston. She would move multiple times to different parts of the country.

Killers do not like to leave eyewitnesses behind. It was certainly understandable that Webb lived in fear that her assailant might one day return to finish the job. Years would go by, and then Webb looked herself in the mirror one day and decided that enough was enough. "I'm glad you found me," she said.

She now refuses to let her mystery attacker control the rest of her life. "I just decided that I cannot and I will not live in any type of fear any longer."

And she has not. Fully determined to live life to its fullest, Webb has packed her bags and traveled the world. Off to the California coast to see the Big Sur where she hiked between the ocean and the mountains. Off to the Midwest and Mackinac Island, visiting the walled cluster of military buildings from the 1700s. And then her dream, off to Paris to visit the Notre Dame Cathedral, see the sights, and celebrate the new freedom she had found.

After you have beaten death, as Vicki Webb has learned, there is a wonderful, glorious life to live. And she is living it to the fullest, assailant be damned. "This whole ordeal has been both a blessing and a curse at the same time for me and my family," Vicki said. "It has certainly been a horrible curse for me to endure, the surgeries and the rehab and the daily side effects that I still live with every day, that is for sure. But I do not block it out of my mind or out of my memory. I am not in any kind of denial by any means. I know exactly what happened to me that day. This horrible thing happened to me, Vicki

Webb. But it has also been an amazing, incredible blessing for my entire family, who thought they were going to lose me, and to see me recover, and for me now being able to move forward with the rest of my life. It has become much more important for me to live a regular life now. So many blessings have come out of that terrible, horrible day, and that is what I choose to focus on going forward with the rest of my life. I am focused on the blessings, and not the horribleness of it."

Vicki paused. Then said, "That man took a lot of my life away from me on that day. And once I made the choice that he could not have any more of my life, I have never looked back. Not once."

CHAPTER 24
"I would recognize that voice of his. To this day, I would definitely recognize his voice..."

Like Vicki Webb, investigators do not know if the three Texas shooting locations, and Vicki's assailant, are connected to the I-70 killings. They are certainly similar. But if indeed they are one in the same, the killer of Mary Ann Glasscock in Fort Worth and Amy Vess in Arlington, and the attempted killing of Vicki Webb in Houston had changed his choice of guns. And thus the ballistics do not match.

With a year off between the killings, the murderer simply could have put the old gun away in favor of a new one, especially after police told him they knew what gun he was using.

"I consider myself very, very lucky," Vicki Webb said. "If indeed I was a part of the I-70 killings, I am the ninth victim. The other eight before me are no longer with us. But whether I was part of the I-70 case or not part of the I-70 case, there still was somebody who tried to kill me, and if that person is still alive today, he is still out there, and he needs to be caught."

And Vicki is now content and determined to be front and center in the pursuit of the gunman. She has since traveled to Washington DC to meet with a team of FBI agents investigating the case. She is keeping in touch with an FBI agent near her home. She has seen the composite sketches of the I-70 killer, and has compared them to her attacker many times in her mind.

"The composite was very similar to the man I remember. I can tell there were similarities. But I would never say that was exactly him. For me, it is more his voice that I remember than his face. I would recognize that voice of his. To this day, I would definitely recognize his voice."

I told Vicki I had something for her to see. "If it is a scary movie, they don't bother me anymore." She laughed.

With that, I shared the Billy Brossman convenience store tape, which she had never seen. She watched it intently. "I can't really hear enough of his voice," she said. "The volume is low."

She kept watching, as the killer walked Brossman to the back of the room. "The age, the height... maybe." She paused. "But otherwise, this guy does not look like the guy who shot me."

Vicki kept watching, looking for a connection. She said, "But I would never say never. Thirty years is a long time. I wish I could hear his voice better."

Vicki says she understands the fascination with the I-70 case, and if the I-70 case is connected to her, then she is the lone survivor of his killing spree. But she has become able to go through with her life without being consumed by it. "I have followed the I-70 case in the past over the years, but I do not choose to live there anymore. After a while, yes, this horrible thing did happen to me. But there is a whole entire life outside of that day. I think it was just my choice to remain ignorant as to the I-70 investigation, and leave it be in my mind. I originally did what I could to help, but I chose not to be that involved. It was just not a place that I wanted to live." She paused again. "We all make a choice of what we choose to do each and every day. I have chosen to move on and live my life as normally as I possibly can."

That is not to say that she is not hoping for a resolution someday. Far from it. And if that day ever comes, she will be ready. "This person needs to be caught. This person needs to be taken off of the streets. I just want him off the streets. If he is out there, he needs to be taken into custody. He needs to be treated. He needs to be held accountable for all of his actions. He is a sick, sick human being. Evil. Pure evil."

And if her assailant is caught, Vicki Webb says she wants to be there to confront him, and look him in the eye. "I want to ask him why. Why did he feel the need to do this? He was driven in some way. It is the psychology of it. Why? Why did he choose me? What happened in his life that truly made this an okay thing for him to do?"

Of course, she already knows the answers: "I know there are no answers for those questions."

And if the day does ever come, she says she will confront her attacker in court, to show him that she won. "I would not even be fearful sitting across from him. My fear of him is long gone."

For Vicki Webb, however, no matter how this saga ends, there will never be closure. "Closure? I am not even looking for closure. I am not even looking for an apology. I just want him caught."

She believes, just like the detectives in Indianapolis, Wichita, Terre Haute, St. Charles, Raytown, Fort Worth, Arlington, and Houston do, that the answer will probably need to come from within. "I would like to think his family turns him in, or a neighbor turns him in," she said. "I want him off the streets so nobody else goes through what me and my family went through. Others have lost loved ones. I am very lucky. Get this horrible human being off the streets so he cannot do this to anyone else."

With that, I knew I had pushed her far enough. She had spilled her soul to a complete stranger in hopes that it might someday, some way, help locate the man who left her for dead.

We left the restaurant, got in the car, and headed to the airport, just the two of us, strangers until I made that random phone call. Now suddenly friends, brought together by an event 30 years earlier. We both found the irony in that.

We drove through the rain in silence for a few minutes. "You now know my life story, Bob," she finally said.

I could only nod. "When you tell them my story," she said, "you tell them that I am no longer afraid."

I said I would.

We parked the car, shook hands, and said goodbye. "Vicki Webb," I said, "You are one incredible lady."

She waved me off and I watched her head toward the door, then turn back at me one last time. "You know, Bob," she said, "I am not really that tough of a cookie."

I laughed. "Now you are lying," I said.

CHAPTER 25

"There are several times I just think we are a million miles away and there are other times I think we are very close to getting somewhere on this..."

In Florida at DNA Labs International, the results began to slowly trickle in. It is not cheap. FBI grants are helping.

No match yet on Robin Fuldauer's clothes from Indianapolis.

No match yet on the wedding veil from Wichita.

No match yet on Mick McCown's pants from Terre Haute.

No match yet on Nancy Kitzmiller's pants from St. Charles.

No match yet on Sarah Blessing's clothes from Raytown.

The testing has now moved onto shell casings.

The answers that the task force hoped for did not come. For investigators, with fresh homicide cases piling up on their desks, it was a bitter pill to swallow. In Indianapolis, Detective Columbus Ricks can only shake his head in frustration. "All we can do is keep digging," he said.

His partner David Ellison, ready to retire, is left pondering the families' pain. "Closure is an overrated term. Although families may someday have good answers, it still does not take away the pain of missing their loved one. I am just hoping that is where we can get to someday."

Susan Fuldauer is hoping along with them. But even if there is a resolution in her sister's case someday, it will only go so far. "We have never just had a level of acceptance, a level of being able to move on."

They won't be forgetting, or forgiving anytime soon in Wichita.

Some people feel the I-70 killer is already dead, or perhaps sitting behind bars. For some, that will be enough punishment. But not for Ruth Feather, Patricia Smith's friend. "To be very honest with you, I hope he is still alive because I want to see him punished severely. I want to live long enough to see that happen."

And for Patricia Magers' husband Mark, do not use the word closure. That will never happen. "There is never going to be any closure for me. I just try to live one day at a time and move on. I think about this daily. Not a day of my life that this has not haunted me and I know it will until the day I die. I want her back. And I know that will never happen."

You can still hear the pain in Norm Smith's voice, as he searches for the right words to describe the loss of his wife Patricia. "Even today, I feel like there is a part of me that is missing. It never gets any better."

In Terre Haute, forgetting about the case is also not an option. "I think it is in you. If you are an investigator, it is in you," said Police Chief Shawn Keen. "It is something you just can't set aside, and you can't stop thinking about it when you go home."

Terre Haute Detective Troy Davis was a young patrolman on the day Michael McCown was murdered on Highway 41. He has held the case file in his lap for many years. Davis says his feelings for the victim and their families is what keeps pushing him forward. "Once you have contact with that family, that is your motivation to keep moving on. You keep working these cases until you are unable to work them anymore. If you are an investigator it is in your blood. You can't just set it aside when you go home at night."

For the families, there is always hope that someday, somehow, there might be an answer. But it will never be enough, no matter what DNA results may someday bring. "I miss him so very much," Cynthia Brock says about her brother Mick. "Our family just gave up having any hope to solve this case a long time ago. I just want this nightmare to be finally over with. I want whoever did this to be caught and punished. If they could finally catch him, it would mean so much to our family. It would mean the world to all of us."

And her sister Teresa agreed. "Nothing will ever bring him back. That is all I really ever wanted. Sure, I would like to see whoever did this punished, but there is no closure for our family. And there never will be."

For Brad Rumsey, retirement called and he turned in his badge. But he has not turned the page on the I-70 killer. "No chance," Rumsey said when I tracked him down on the phone. He is still helping out with the prosecuting attorney's office, and "playing bad golf." He laughed.

Before saying goodbye, I asked Rumsey if he had any final thoughts as I prepared to write the book. "There has been a six-pack of beer sitting in our evidence room for more than 20 years," he said. "The Billy Brossman beer. We could not pull prints then. But maybe we can pull DNA now."

There was a pause, and I waited for what I long suspected Rumsey thought, but could not say while wearing the badge. "Because Bob, in my mind, the Brossman killer is the I-70 killer."

In St. Charles, Don Stepp has traded in his badge for a fishing pole. Stepp is a quiet and reserved man. Like many police detectives, he can be hard to read, keeping his cards close to his vest. As professional a homicide detective as you could find, he has taken the case personally, and has taken it home with him. "I would be lying to you if I told you I did not think about this case all of the time. There have been times when I am just driving down Highway 70, when some old lead just pops up in my mind. The Nancy Kitzmiller case is always with me. When I am thinking about this case and all of the leads that have been done and all of the what if's and what could we have done or what did we do right or what did we do wrong, there are several times I just think we are a million miles away and there are other times I think we are very close to getting somewhere on this."

Give up on finding the killer? You have not met Raymond Floyd. The man who started the task force has found chasing the I-70 killer a habit he has no desire to break. "I am doing something on this case every single day I am at work. We haven't given up on this case. All it takes is one break."

The last guy standing on the case, no matter how bleak, will be the grizzled gentleman from St. Charles, Patrick McCarrick. "We have never put this case on the shelf. I promise you we never will."

And the case now sits in the lap of Kelly Rhodes, born just after the I-70 killer struck. She knows what is at stake. "I definitely feel a lot of responsibility to be given something like this."

And besides the families, perhaps no one has been more tortured by the case than the quiet gentleman from Raytown, Tim Hickman. "It has bothered me for 30 years," Hickman said, trying unsuccessfully to hold back tears. "Did I do enough? Did I act fast enough? If I had not waited so long, they might have caught him. I did not want to cause a panic for everyone. I just tried to do the best I could."

And after all this time, Mike Crooke, the first detective on the scene, a man of incredible patience, is also haunted by frustration. "I just can't imagine that we have not somehow, somewhere, some way, stumbled on to somebody, someone that may be a prime suspect and for some reason we do not realize it, or why hasn't somebody from the public come forward on this terrible thing? It is so horrendous, you would think somebody has to know something about this, and would feel obligated to pick up the phone, do the right thing, and call the police."

And whether or not the day comes with a resolution to the I-70 serial killer, Vicki Webb continues to move forward. To do so, she has played a little trick on herself. "I choose in my mind to think that he is dead. Maybe that makes life a little easier for me. But he will have no effect on me. He has had enough of my life. He can't have any more. I choose not to give it to him." Vicki Webb has since listened with the FBI to the enhanced voice on the Billy Brossman tape. She does not believe the Brossman killer was her assailant.

And after all the investigations, and all the testing, FBI profiler Larry Ankrom knows one thing for certain. "Make no mistake that this guy likes to read and watch all of the television news stories," Ankrom said. "Anything about himself and the murders he wants to consume. He wants to know what the police might know about him. He wants to learn everything there is to know about the case." Ankrom paused. "And if he is still alive, he still does."

Which means he is reading this. May the police someday get lucky.

www.ingramcontent.com/pod-product-compliance
Lightning Source LLC
Chambersburg PA
CBHW062127020426
42335CB00013B/1130